SARAH TIONG'S
MODERN ASIAN

Recipes and Stories from an
Asian-Australian Kitchen

SARAH TIONG'S
MODERN ASIAN

SARAH TIONG

author of *Sweet, Savory, Spicy*

PAGE STREET
PUBLISHING CO.

PAGE STREET
PUBLISHING CO.

Copyright © 2023 Sarah Tiong

First published in 2023 by
Page Street Publishing Co.
27 Congress Street, Suite 1511
Salem, MA 01970
www.pagestreetpublishing.com

Distributed by Macmillan, sales in Canada by The Canadian Manda Group.

27 26 25 24 23 1 2 3 4 5

ISBN-13: 978-1-64567-733-8
ISBN-10: 1-64567-733-8

Library of Congress Control Number: 2022945419

Cover and book design by Meg Baskis for Page Street Publishing Co.
Photography by Ben Cole

Printed and bound in the United States

DEDICATION

For Mum. You are my heart and home.

May every dish I make share a little of your love, until we're together again.

CONTENTS

SOMETHING LIGHT   68

SOMETHING SWEET   102

SNACKS + SIDES   124

INTRODUCTION

Up until now, I've kept this pretty private. Just a few months after the conclusion of my last appearance on *MasterChef Australia* in 2020, I lost my mum. It is the toughest, most painful journey I've ever embarked on. This book is in honour of her and the lessons she taught me in the kitchen and in the aisles of the grocery stores. It's a book of thanks to the ingredients she raised me on, discovered with me and encouraged me to try at least once. My curiosity, my passion and my commitment are all thanks to the woman she was.

Mum was only a teenager when she left the sticky humidity of Sarawak, Malaysia, and landed in red-brick-lined, skyscraper-dotted, sandy beach–spotted Sydney, Australia. She had never lived without her own parents before and had never learnt to cook. Soon, she found herself running her own business seven days a week and raising two kids who seemed to eat like vacuums. Suddenly "rice and fried eggs" didn't cut it and her babies were begging for spaghetti and meatballs, lasagne, roast dinners and endless snacks that she'd never cooked or tasted before. So, what was a busy woman on a budget to do when all she had in her pantry were soy sauce, sesame oil, fish sauce and a little bit of miso? She found inspiration anywhere she could; she took bold guesses and made a few mistakes along the way, but it soon became a glorious creative world of deliciousness and joy.

It's all led to this book; recipes focused on maximum flavour from a staple Asian pantry as an homage to the incredible cuisine my mother devised, with my own modern take on it. The recipes are not authentic or traditional Asian recipes—they are things like spaghetti and meatballs made with miso paste and fish sauce that are the most umami-packed plate of comfort, roast chickens slathered in Thai red curry paste, picnic sandwiches stuffed to the brim with sticky *charsiu*, pickles and coleslaw. My mother was Chinese-Malaysian. I'm Chinese-Malaysian-Australian and that has a huge impact on the food I eat. Layer that with all the nuances of being time poor, having a small budget every day and learning to cook on your own, and you get food that is all about heart and emotion. All the recipes in this book are about innovation and a little left-of-field cooking, without compromising on taste.

This book reflects the way I love to eat and cook. There aren't any hard or fast rules, I'm not always bound to tradition and, to me, authenticity is subjective. I want flavour, texture, lightness, richness, boldness, subtleness and every nuance in between. I want food that speaks to memories, emotion, curiosity, bravery, fun and drawing the best out of ingredients. As a chef, I fell in love with French and Italian cuisine early on. They felt exotic, elegant and dreamy. The pursuit of technique and process motivated me. But as I developed as a chef, my heart always gravitated home, towards Southeast Asian comfort. But the creative excitement and passion really blossomed when I found ways to play in all fields, borrowing flavours from Southeast Asian cuisine and blending them with techniques and aesthetics of French and Italian cuisine. I hope these recipes surprise and delight you as much as they have for me.

I've poured a lot of my grief, memories and love into this book. My food comes from humble beginnings but has landed in a very emotional, conscientious place worthy of being my career and passion.

PANTRY + SAUCES

This chapter is your powerhouse of flavour. This is the same pantry my mother kept when I was growing up. I've inherited the same sauces and condiments, from Green Sauce (page 19) to Ponzu Sauce (page 24) to Sweet + Sour Tamarind Sauce (page 20) and so many things in between. From these basic ingredients, the world of possibility is vast. There is no limit to the creativity you can apply to these ingredients. I'll give you a full explanation of the pantry and give you several sauce recipes that are used throughout the subsequent chapters as bases and extra layers of flavour. Use this as a starting point to build your own Asian pantry and get excited by the deliciousness you collect and create.

PANTRY STAPLES

Chinese Five-Spice Powder

According to traditional Chinese medicine, Chinese five-spice is based on the five elements of fire, water, wood, earth and metal. These elements are manifested in different parts of the body and require careful balance to promote health and energy, hence the creation of this spice mix. The spices are star anise, fennel seeds, Szechuan peppercorns, clove and cinnamon. It is wonderfully aromatic, warm, Christmassy and extremely versatile. I've used it in sauces, mains and even desserts.

Dark Soy Sauce (Mushroom Flavoured)

The brand my family has favoured most, and one that I've had the pleasure of working with briefly, is Lee Kum Kee. In particular, I am a huge fan of their mushroom-flavoured dark soy sauce. It adds colour and umami without being as salty as light soy sauce. If you can't find mushroom-flavoured dark soy sauce, simply use any dark soy sauce you can find.

Maggi Seasoning

This is a very savoury sauce I grew up with. We added it to everything from congee and eggs to dumplings and salads. This seasoning is heavy on the salt, but it provides an extreme amount of umami. It's like if light soy sauce and chicken bouillon had a baby, then added MSG to it.

Mirin

This is a sweet sake used to add sweetness and depth to a dish without adding heaviness. Mirin is fantastic for adding sweet aromas to sauces and marinades. By adding mirin, you're essentially adding the sugar from the alcohol, which helps with caramelisation of meats and vegetables.

Oyster Sauce

This is actually made from oysters, but you can find vegan or vegetarian versions. Oyster sauce adds sweetness, saltiness and thickness. It comes out of the bottle thick and glossy. This makes it perfect for stir-fries. It's also fantastic as a base for marinades and other sauces.

Kewpie Mayonnaise (Japanese Mayonnaise)

Another iconic brand I grew up with is Kewpie Mayonnaise. It's more savoury than Western mayonnaise and has the perfect texture. It isn't gluey or tacky; it is perfectly creamy. It can be piped, it can be dolloped and best of all, it adds a fantastic body to any sauce. It's perfect for dipping fried foods into or using as a binder for coleslaw.

Chinkiang Vinegar (Black Vinegar)

This Chinese vinegar has a very distinct flavour. It is savoury with an acidity that warms the back of your throat. A little goes a long way. If I had to compare it to anything, it's like apple cider vinegar mixed with Worcestershire sauce and a dash of light soy sauce. It's extremely good for fatty cuts of meat and dressings.

Cooking Sake

Similar to mirin, this adds sweetness and depth. However, it's a little more bitter and alcoholic. This Japanese cooking alcohol is perfect for braising or stewing meats in, adding to marinades and using for cures in seafood. There is no saltiness to this condiment, so it needs to be added along with something salty.

Fish Sauce

This is one of the must-have staples. There is no replacement for this, other than perhaps a vegetarian or vegan version (but it still won't be the same). Fish sauce adds saltiness, umami and funkiness to a dish. It is a little pungent and a little stinky—very similar to liquid MSG. It is to Southeast Asians what anchovies and Parmigiano-Reggiano is to Italians. It builds complexity and it makes everything taste just a little better.

Lao Gan Ma Crispy Chilli Oil

This is my absolute favourite chilli oil in the world. It has crispy soybeans in it, a wonderful tingly spice, and it is full of richness and texture. I use this in everything: marinades, sauces, as a way to dress dishes; sometimes I even just eat a spoonful of it on steamed rice or mix it through cooked spaghetti. It is wonderfully versatile and tasty.

ABC Chilli Sauce

This is better than Sriracha, in my opinion. It is spicier, and has a better consistency and a great vibrant colour. This sauce is amazing in marinades for ribs and chicken wings. I also add it to noodles, soups, stir-fries and fried rice.

Miso

This is Japanese fermented soybeans, famous for making miso soup. However, just like any fermented product, its application is extremely versatile. Miso has the most wonderful salty umami. The two most common types of miso are *shiromiso* (white miso) and *akamiso* (red miso). Shiromiso is the most widely produced miso, made mostly of rice, barley and a small quantity of soybeans. If a greater quantity of soybeans were added, the miso would be red or brown. Compared with red miso, white miso has a very short fermentation time and is slightly sweeter and less intense than red miso. Akamiso is aged, sometimes for more than one year. The colour changes over this time to a darker red, and is a more intense miso.

Hoisin Sauce

This sweet and savoury sauce is best known for its application in Peking duck pancakes. But just like oyster sauce, it is wonderful as a base for marinades and dipping sauces. This sauce is sticky and almost syrupy out of the jar. It adds colour and a sweet fragrance to food.

Southeast Asian Curry Pastes

Store-bought red, yellow and green curry pastes are always handy to have in the pantry. These pastes should not be seen as only useful for making curries. They offer a huge amount of concentrated flavour perfect for marinades, stir-fries and even soups. My advice is to try a few different brands and find the one you like best. Other curry pastes you might consider include *rendang*, *panang* and *assam*.

Sesame Oil

This is the crown jewel of oils. What an extraordinary extra virgin olive oil is to the European world, sesame oil is to Chinese cooking. The subtle smokiness, nuttiness and silky texture is heralded in high-quality sesame oils. A little goes a long way. This is a powerful flavoured oil that can be used in anything from dipping sauces to ice cream bases.

GREEN SAUCE

My mother inherited her mastery of sauces from her father—a skill that I think developed because of the simplicity of the food she ate growing up. A lot of it was steamed, raw or boiled. The sauces really brought life and vibrancy to Mum's food. Even though Mum grew to discover and love braising, stir-frying and grilling, she always made a phenomenal sauce to go with it. This punchy, herby sauce goes well with everything, particularly bolder, richer flavours of heavy spice or deep-fried dishes, or even stirred through pasta or potato salad. The acidity and herbaceousness really creates harmony.

Time: 10 minutes | Makes: approximately 2 AUS cups or 500 ml or 2 US cups + 2 US tbsp

75 to 100 g (2.5 to 3.5 oz) fresh coriander (cilantro) with roots attached (approximately ½ bunch)

75 to 100 g (2.5 to 3.5 oz) fresh flat-leaf parsley (approximately ½ bunch)

3 green serrano chillies, roughly chopped

2 to 3 spring onions, roughly chopped

4 to 5 cloves garlic, peeled

½ AUS cup or 125 ml or ½ US cup + 1 tsp white vinegar

3 AUS tbsp or 60 ml or ¼ US cup fish sauce

9 g (2 tsp) caster (superfine) sugar

1 tsp freshly ground black pepper

⅔ AUS cup or 167 ml or ⅔ US cup + 1½ tsp neutral oil (rice bran, grapeseed, vegetable)

Add the coriander, parsley, green chillies, spring onions, garlic, vinegar, fish sauce, sugar and black pepper to a food processor. Blitz until finely chopped and well combined (approximately 1 minute).

Transfer the herb mixture to a bowl and mix in the oil. This sauce may be stored in a jar or airtight container in the fridge for up to 3 weeks.

TIPS

» You can use a variety of herbs, including mint, basil or shiso.

» You can use a variety of vinegars, including apple cider vinegar, red wine vinegar or sherry vinegar.

SWEET + SOUR TAMARIND SAUCE

Tamarind was featured in a lot of the food I ate while growing up. I saw it in various forms: dried slices made dark and leathery from air-drying to use in soups and braises; packets of sticky, candy-like chewy bars to pinch and tear at for making tamarind water, sauces and drinks; and jars of shiny, thick purée used for sauce bases and marinades. Watching my family use tamarind in so many ways revealed just how full of personality the ingredient is. My uncle's tamarind sauce is slightly sweeter, my aunt's is slightly thinner in texture and my mother's was glossy and aromatic and full of sour punch. This sweet and sour tamarind sauce is very close to my mother's. I never did get the exact recipe from her, so I've re-created it the best I can, and I love that in some way, my own fingerprint has been added to a generational recipe.

Time: 10 minutes | Makes: approximately 2 AUS cups or 250 ml or 2 US cups + 2 US tbsp

2 AUS tbsp or 40 ml or 2 US tbsp + 2 tsp neutral oil (rice bran, vegetable or grapeseed)

2 small red onions, finely diced

8 to 10 cloves garlic, finely minced

4 AUS tbsp or 80 ml or ⅓ US cup tomato sauce (ketchup)

1 AUS tbsp or 20 ml or 4 tsp tomato paste

100 g (3.5 oz) dark brown sugar

220 g (8 oz) tamarind purée

12 g (2 tsp) salt

1 AUS cup or 250 ml or 1 US cup + 2 tsp water

Heat the oil in a large frying pan or wok over medium heat until hot. Then, sauté the onions and garlic for 1 to 2 minutes, until they begin to brown lightly.

Add the tomato sauce, tomato paste, brown sugar, tamarind purée and salt and stir thoroughly for 1 to 2 minutes, until fully incorporated. Add the water, then stir again until combined. Allow to simmer for 3 to 4 minutes, or until reduced to your desired thickness. Taste and adjust the seasoning to your preference.

TIP

» The tomato sauce can be omitted—just increase the tomato paste and brown sugar for more sweetness and tomato flavour.

GARLIC SAUCE

There is a Lebanese-Australian charcoal chicken joint in Sydney called El Jannah that has an almost cult following. Aside from the chicken, the one thing that people will rave about is the garlic sauce called *toum*. It is thick, fluffy, pearly white and pretty much smacks you in the face with garlicky goodness. If there's one ingredient in the world that my family and I can't live without, it's garlic. So, when I discovered toum, it was an absolute revelation. I became obsessed. I probably made over 20 batches of this stuff, desperate to find my ideal balance between the spicy bite of garlic, the lightness and creaminess and the acidic tingle of lemon.

Time: 15 minutes | Makes: 4 to 5 AUS cups or 1 L to 1.25 L or 4¼ to 5¼ US cups

200 g cloves garlic (approximately 1½ AUS or US cups, or 5 to 6 large bulbs), peeled

12 g (2 tsp) salt

4 AUS cups or 1 L or 4¼ US cups neutral oil (rice bran, grapeseed, vegetable)

¾ AUS cup or 187 ml or ¾ US cup + 1½ tsp fresh lemon juice

1 AUS tbsp or 20 ml or 4 tsp ice water

In a food processor, blitz the garlic and salt together, stopping intermittently to scrape the garlic down the sides of the processor, for 3 to 4 minutes, until thoroughly and finely minced.

While the food processor is running, slowly pour 1 teaspoon of the oil into the processor. Allow the processor to run for 10 seconds, then stop and scrape down the sides of the processor. Repeat this process, 1 teaspoon at a time, for another 10 teaspoons (50 ml) of oil, until the garlic starts to thicken and look creamy.

Keep the processor running and now alternate between adding 3 teaspoons (15 ml) of oil and 1 teaspoon of lemon juice, allowing the processor to run for 4 to 5 seconds between each addition, until the oil and lemon juice has been used up and the sauce appears thickened and fluffy. Finally, add the ice water and allow it to fully incorporate. The sauce will become slightly more pearlescent white.

Transfer the sauce to a glass container and cover with a paper towel in the fridge overnight. The next day, replace the paper towel with an airtight lid and keep in the fridge for up to 3 months.

TIPS

» Fresh lemon juice is a must. It has the correct acidity for the emulsion and the best flavour. Don't use bottled lemon juice.

» Be sure to alternate between the oil and lemon juice. Add both these ingredients very slowly. Adding too much at once will break the emulsion and you'll just have super-oily garlicky soup.

» The ice water at the end isn't necessary, but it does create a slightly lighter, brighter sauce.

» Do not use a blender. You could use a small food processor and do small batches, but you want a processor that has an opening to allow you to add oil and lemon juice while it's running.

PONZU

My first introduction to yuzu was by its perfume, wafting gracefully through the air in the ponzu that was served with my order of prawn tempura at a Japanese restaurant tucked away upstairs in a mall along a busy road. I had always thought tempura was served with soy sauce. Suddenly I was faced with this citrusy fragrance, like a delicate mix of lemon, grapefruit and mandarin. I dipped my chopstick into the sauce, gave it a swirl and stuck it in my mouth. The salty soy, the sweet mirin, the oceanic hum of bonito and kombu, and finally the brightness of the yuzu sang the perfect harmony together. While this sauce may look simple, there is depth of flavour and a lightness that means it can (and should) be used to enhance and balance seasoning. I highly recommend using it with tempura, sashimi and very simply grilled ingredients.

Time: 5 minutes | Makes: 1½ AUS cups or 360 ml or 1½ US cups

1 tsp sugar (or to taste)

120 ml (½ US cup) light soy sauce

60 ml (¼ US cup) mirin

60 ml (¼ US cup) sake

15 ml (1 US tbsp) rice vinegar

¼ AUS cup or 3 g or ¼ US cup katsuobushi (bonito flakes)

1 piece kombu, approximately 7.5 cm (3") square

60 ml (¼ US cup) yuzu juice (alternatively, use equal parts fresh lemon and lime juice)

In a small saucepan, bring the sugar, soy sauce, mirin, sake, rice vinegar, katsuobushi and kombu to a boil for 1 minute. Remove from the heat and strain into a sterilised heatproof jar, discarding the solids. Stir in the yuzu juice (or lemon and lime juices) until fully incorporated. Store in the fridge for up to 4 weeks.

TIP

» Ponzu can be used in a variety of ways: as a dipping sauce for sashimi, dumplings, fried chicken or tempura; in marinades for protein and vegetables; or in salad dressings and vinaigrettes.

SOMETHING SUBSTANTIAL

If you're looking for lip-smacking, saucy recipes, this chapter will surely satisfy you. These are what to reach for when you want something hearty, meaty and full of spices or something to comfort you lovingly or inspire you. The dining table is where I put my heart and emotion for everyone to share. It has always been the place where I can connect with people, be my genuine self and express myself. That's why this chapter is all about richer, bigger dishes to share. The flavours hit every note: sweet, sour, salty, spicy, bitter, pungent. Best of all, they combine cuisines from around the world in a way that makes sense, creates layers of deliciousness, results in conversation pieces and uses an array of cooking techniques that are all achievable within home kitchens.

This chapter is where "out-of-left-field" cooking really shines and should inspire you to get creative with curry pastes, sauces, pickles and spices. Some of these recipes even take different cuisines and mash them together to create something truly tasty. That's what I want you to walk away with: don't follow rules, just create something delicious.

THAI RED CURRY ROAST CHICKEN

Curry pastes are not just for curries. They should be thought of as flavour bombs, concentrated pastes to be used in marinades, sauces, vinaigrettes and stir-fries. Your pantry should be well stocked with a variety of curry pastes. For me, Thai curry pastes by Maesri are reliable. It is also about the condiments you add to it, like fish sauce, lime juice, sugar or shrimp paste. These curry pastes should be used with curiosity and gusto whether you're grilling meat, seafood, making fried rice, salad dressings or even pasta! This roast chicken recipe is a great first step into the world of possibilities with curry pastes and demonstrates how the addition of a little coconut milk, fish sauce and lime can create complexity and balance to the humble roast chicken.

Time: 1 hour 10 minutes + 30 minutes marinating | Makes: 4 to 6 servings

MARINADE

2 to 3 AUS tbsp or 40 to 60 g or 2⅔ to 4 US tbsp Thai red curry paste (see Tips)

2 AUS tbsp or 40 ml or 2 US tbsp + 2 tsp fish sauce

Juice of 1 lime

6 g (2 tsp) garlic powder, or 4 cloves garlic, minced

1 tsp freshly ground black pepper

½ AUS cup or 125 ml or ½ US cup + 1 tsp full-fat coconut milk

2 AUS tbsp or 40 ml or 2 US tbsp + 2 tsp neutral oil

1 (2 kg [4½-lb]) chicken

SERVING

Fresh Thai basil leaves

Fresh coriander (cilantro) leaves

Fresh dill leaves

Fresh mint leaves

Steamed rice

Mix together all the marinade ingredients in a bowl until the oil and coconut milk are completely incorporated. Set aside.

Remove the excess fat from the cavity of the chicken. Then, cut down one side of the backbone. Lay the chicken out flat, bone side down. Place your hand on the breast of the chicken, pressing down firmly until it cracks, to butterfly or spatchcock the chicken.

Spread the marinade over the chicken, coating both sides. Let the chicken marinate for at least 30 minutes. Overnight in the fridge gives best results.

Preheat the oven to 180°C (350°F). Place the chicken on a rack over a lined tray. Then, roast the chicken for 70 minutes. Once roasted, remove from the heat and transfer the chicken to a serving platter. Let the chicken rest for at least 20 minutes.

Serve the whole chicken garnished generously with Thai basil, coriander, dill and mint leaves. Best eaten with steamed rice.

TIPS

» I recommend Maesri Thai curry pastes for authentic flavour and consistency.

» This recipe would work with other types of curry pastes, such as green curry, panang curry and massaman curry.

» You could remove the entire backbone of the chicken when butterflying, but I find that leaving the backbone on gives an extra bit of crispy skin at the end, and produces less waste. Typically the bishop's nose (tail) is also eaten.

» This recipe works well with drumsticks, too. Roast drumsticks for 45 minutes, rotating halfway through the roasting time.

BRAISED PORK BELLY + PASSIONFRUIT

This may seem really odd, but one of my favourite combinations commonly found in Thailand is passionfruit and fish sauce. The sweet and sour pulp is tamed by the salty fish sauce and creates the most mouth-watering pairing. This pork belly dish features generous usage of pungent fish sauce and dark soy sauce and borrows an Italian technique of melting anchovy fillets into the sauce to create intense umami. There is no overwhelming fishiness. The final dressing of fresh passionfruit pulp lifts the flavours; the tropical acidity cuts the richness of sticky pork fat and heavily savoury sauce. This is comfort in a bowl.

Time: 1½ to 2 hours | Makes: 4 servings

450 g (16 oz) pork belly, skin on

2 tinned anchovy fillets

1 AUS tbsp or 20 ml or 4 tsp oil from tinned anchovies

1 medium-sized brown onion, finely diced

5 cloves garlic, lightly crushed

3 dried red bird's-eye chillies

1 star anise

1 cinnamon quill (stick)

2 AUS tbsp or 40 ml or 2 US tbsp + 2 tsp mushroom-flavoured dark soy sauce

1 AUS tbsp or 20 ml or 4 tsp fish sauce

1 AUS tbsp or 20 ml or 4 tsp Chinkiang black vinegar

2 AUS cups or 500 ml or 2 US cups + 2 US tbsp water

2 AUS tbsp or 40 g or 2 US tbsp + 2 tsp dark brown sugar

Juice and pulp of 2 passionfruit

SERVING

Steamed rice

Noodles

Slice the pork belly into 5-cm (2-inch) squares and set aside. Place a large saucepan over medium-high heat. Once hot, add the anchovies and anchovy oil. Stir-fry until the anchovy fillets begin to break down.

Add the onion and garlic. Stir-fry for 2 to 3 minutes, or until the onion is lightly golden. Then, add the pork belly and stir-fry for a further 2 to 3 minutes, or until the pork is lightly browned.

Add the dried chilli, star anise, cinnamon quill, soy sauce, fish sauce and black vinegar to the pork. Stir-fry for a further 2 to 3 minutes. Then, add the water and brown sugar, mix well and bring to a boil. Once boiling, lower the heat to medium-low. Allow to simmer for 1 hour to 90 minutes, or until the pork is soft and tender and the sauce has reduced significantly to a sticky consistency.

Transfer the pork to a serving bowl. Dress liberally with passionfruit pulp and juice. Serve with steamed rice or noodles.

TIP

» The seasoning can be adjusted by adding more water to dilute saltiness or more fish sauce to increase saltiness.

QUICK
PEACH KALBI
(Korean-Style Beef Short Ribs)
+ PA MUCHIM
(Spring Onion Salad)

Korean barbecue is probably one of my family's most favourite options for dining out. During my teenage years, it was something that was considered expensive and so we didn't get to have it often. Now that I'm an adult, and Korean barbecue is probably one of the most popular food choices in Australia, it's much more commonplace amongst my friends and family. The combination of *kalbi* and *pa muchim* (spring onion salad) is big and bold. There is something about the peppery spring onion and the sweet marinade that awakens the appetite. Combined with rice and perilla leaf, it is a gorgeous bite. Wanting to re-create the experience at home, I searched for ingredients to make my kalbi marinade. Korean pears being out of season, I gambled with the idea of a sweet and tart peach. The acidity helps tenderise the short ribs and the result is a fruity, balanced marinade.

Time: 4 to 12 hours marinating, 40 minutes cooking | Makes: 4 servings

KALBI

10 cloves garlic

2 peaches, stones removed

1 small brown onion

1 (2.5-cm [1"]) piece fresh ginger, peeled and coarsely chopped

½ AUS cup or 125 ml or ½ US cup + 1 tsp mirin

½ AUS cup or 125 ml or ½ US cup + 1 tsp light soy sauce

½ AUS cup or 125 g or ½ US cup + 2 US tbsp sugar

60 ml (¼ US cup) toasted sesame oil

1 tsp freshly ground black pepper

1.1 kg (2½ lb) 6-mm to 1.5-cm (¼" to ½") thick butterflied bone-in beef short ribs (see Tips)

For the kalbi, blitz the garlic, peaches, onion and ginger to a smooth purée in a food processor or blender. Add the mirin, soy sauce, sugar, sesame oil and black pepper. Blitz again for 2 to 3 minutes, or until the sugar has dissolved and the mixture is smooth.

Place the short ribs in a resealable plastic bag or baking dish. Pour the peach marinade over the ribs and turn the ribs to coat thoroughly. Seal or cover and marinate for a minimum of 4 hours (maximum of 12 hours) in the fridge.

(continued)

TIPS

» You can request your butcher to butterfly the short ribs so that you have one long strip of meat attached to each bone. Alternatively, use flanken or "LA Kalbi" cut ribs.

» The ribs can be marinated and frozen for up to 4 weeks.

» Pre-sliced and curled spring onions can sometimes be found in Korean grocery stores.

PA MUCHIM
(SPRING ONION SALAD)

10 to 12 spring onions (scallions), cut into 7.5-cm (3") pieces

1 AUS tbsp or 20 ml or 4 tsp white vinegar

1 AUS tbsp or 20 ml or 4 tsp mirin

1 tsp gochugaru (coarse Korean red pepper powder)

½ tsp sugar

9 g (1½ tsp) salt

10 ml (2 tsp) sesame oil

1 AUS tbsp or 11 g or 4 tsp toasted white sesame seeds

SERVING

1 large head green, red oak leaf or Bibb lettuce, leaves separated

30 perilla (shiso) leaves

Cooked short-grain rice

Kimchi

In the meantime, for the pa muchim, slice the spring onion pieces lengthwise into very thin strips. Transfer the strips to a large bowl of ice water and let them soak for 10 minutes. Agitate the scallions vigorously with your hand to rinse well and then drain very well and pat dry with paper towels. Place the spring onions in a dry mixing bowl.

In a separate small bowl, mix together the vinegar, mirin, gochugaru, sugar, salt and sesame oil until the sugar and salt are dissolved. Pour this dressing over the spring onions and scatter the sesame seeds on top. Toss the spring onions to coat.

Preheat a grill to a medium-high heat, or place a griddle pan over medium-high heat on the stove. Remove the short ribs from the marinade, shaking off any excess. Then, grill the ribs for 3 to 4 minutes on each side. You want bits of charring and good caramelisation. Rest the ribs on the serving platter for 5 to 6 minutes. Then, use scissors or kitchen shears to cut the meat into bite-sized pieces.

Serve the ribs with the spring onion salad, fresh lettuce and perilla leaves, rice and kimchi. Wrap a piece of the ribs, a mouthful of rice and kimchi in a perilla leaf and lettuce leaf to enjoy maximum flavour.

BAHARAT BEEF SHORT RIBS, SWEET + NUTTY GRAIN SALAD

Middle Eastern cuisines are some of my favourites. Lebanese food, in particular, has always been close to my heart, having grown up with many Lebanese friends. I can draw many similarities between the Lebanese families I know and my own. The approach to food and flavour is common ground. The spirit of family, sharing and generosity seasons each dish and fills the dining table. In Chinese cuisine, we have the signature five-spice blend. In Lebanese cuisine, there is a signature seven-spice blend called *baharat*, generally made up of allspice, black pepper, cinnamon, cloves, coriander seed, cumin and nutmeg. Of course, each family will have their own specific blend, but the one that I've found to give the most aroma and potency is equal parts of each spice. Baharat creates an incredible crust and really does flavour the beef ribs all the way through. I've added soy sauce and fish sauce to help with colouring the ribs and also provide another layer of tastiness and seasoning. The beef ribs are just as much the star of this recipe as the grain salad, which is full of texture, sweetness and lightness.

Time: 4 hours marinating + 2½ hours cooking | Makes: 4 to 6 servings

BAHARAT

2 AUS tbsp or 16 g or 2 US tbsp + 2 tsp ground allspice

2 AUS tbsp or 16 g or 2 US tbsp + 2 tsp freshly ground black pepper

2 AUS tbsp or 19 g or 2 US tbsp + 2 tsp ground cinnamon

2 AUS tbsp or 18 g or 2 US tbsp + 2 tsp ground cloves

2 AUS tbsp or 16 g or 2 US tbsp + 2 tsp ground coriander seed

2 AUS tbsp or 19 g or 2 US tbsp + 2 tsp ground cumin

2 AUS tbsp or 19 g or 2 US tbsp + 2 tsp ground nutmeg

MARINADE

1 AUS tbsp or 20 ml or 4 tsp light soy sauce

1 AUS tbsp or 20 ml or 4 tsp fish sauce

4 AUS tbsp or 80 ml or ⅓ US cup olive oil

For the baharat, in a medium-sized mixing bowl, combine all the baharat spices, whisking thoroughly. Put away half of the mixture in a jar, resealable bag or airtight container for use in another recipe. To the remaining spices, add the marinade ingredients: the soy sauce, fish sauce and olive oil. Whisk until fully incorporated.

Place the ribs in a resealable plastic bag or in a large container. Pour the marinade over the meat and massage into the meat. Allow to marinate for at least 4 hours. This can be prepared 48 hours in advance.

Preheat the oven to 180°C (350°F).

In a heavy, lidded saucepan or pot over medium-high heat, sear the ribs on all sides for 1 to 2 minutes per side. Turn the ribs meat side up, then add the garlic bulb, beef stock and fish sauce. Bring to a boil. Then, place the lid on the pot and transfer the pot to the oven. Braise for 2½ hours, or until fork-tender.

(continued)

TIPS

»   The marinade and grain salad would work perfectly with a roast beef, pork or chicken.

»   Different seeds, nuts and dried fruits can be used in the salad.

SHORT RIBS

8 bone-in short ribs (approximately 250 g [9 oz] each)

1 bulb (whole head) garlic, sliced in half

2 AUS cups or 500 ml or 2 US cups + 2 US tbsp beef stock

2 AUS tbsp or 40 ml or 2 US tbsp + 2 tsp fish sauce

GRAIN SALAD

1 AUS cup or 193 g or 1 US cup + 1½ tsp freekeh or cracked wheat

1 AUS cup or 208 g or 1 US cup + 2 tsp pearl barley

4 AUS tbsp or 37 g or 4 US tbsp + ½ tsp toasted pumpkin seeds

4 AUS tbsp or 29 g or 4 US tbsp + ½ tsp toasted slivered almonds

4 AUS tbsp or 38 g or 4 US tbsp + ½ tsp toasted pine nuts

½ AUS cup or 78 g or ½ US cup + 1 tsp golden raisins

½ AUS cup or 68 g or ½ US cup + 1 tsp finely chopped dried apricots

4 AUS tbsp or 80 ml or ⅓ US cup + ½ tsp Green Sauce (page 19)

3 AUS tbsp or 60 ml or ¼ US cup honey

3 AUS tbsp or 60 ml or ¼ US cup olive oil

SERVING

Garlic Sauce (page 23)

With about 45 minutes remaining on the beef ribs, begin the grain salad: In separate pots, or in one pot one after the other, boil the freekeh and pearl barley in salted boiling water until tender and just cooked through. See the packet instructions for guidance on timing. Drain the cooked grains with a sieve, then onto a clean tea towel to absorb any excess moisture.

Once dry and cooled, transfer the grains to a large mixing bowl along with the pumpkin seeds, almonds, pine nuts, raisins and apricots. Mix well.

In a separate small mixing bowl, mix together the green sauce, honey and olive oil. Mix thoroughly, then pour this dressing over the grain salad. Toss to combine.

Serve the ribs on top of a generous pile of the grain salad and spoon the garlic sauce over the ribs.

ROASTED RENDANG PUMPKIN + COCONUT

This vegetarian dish delivers on flavour, texture and satisfaction. It is relatively quick and a celebration of very simple ingredients coming together to create complexity. Beef rendang is the hallmark slow-cooked dish in Malaysian and Indonesian cuisine. In fact, my very own recipe for rendang paste and the complete beef dish is in my first cookbook, *Sweet, Savory, Spicy*. But in my personal household, rendang paste is not just for stewing into a sauce. I use rendang paste for marinating and slow-roasting lamb shoulders, quick tofu stir-fries, roast vegetables and even for fried rice. This rendang pumpkin is one of my favourites. The pickled onion and texture of shredded coconut really brings the whole dish together and makes it feel like more of a meal.

Time: 1 hour | Makes: 4 servings

PUMPKIN AND COCONUT

1 kg (2¼ lb) pumpkin, peeled, deseeded and cut unto 2.5-cm (1") cubes

150 g (½ US cup + 2 US tbsp) rendang curry paste

1 AUS tbsp or 20 ml or 4 tsp fish sauce

2 AUS tbsp or 40 ml or 2 US tbsp + 2 tsp neutral oil

1 AUS cup or 90 g or 1 US cup + 1 US tbsp shredded coconut

PICKLED RED ONIONS AND CHILLIES

1 AUS cup or 250 ml or 1 US cup + 2 tsp white vinegar

9 g (2 tsp) caster (superfine) sugar

1 red onion, finely sliced

2 red serrano chillies, finely sliced

SALTED COCONUT CREAM

4 AUS tbsp or 80 ml or ⅓ US cup coconut cream

½ tsp salt

SERVING

Makrut lime zest

Toasted walnuts, lightly crushed

Steamed rice or grilled flatbreads (optional)

Preheat the oven to 200°C (400°F).

Begin the pumpkin and coconut: Place the diced pumpkin, rendang paste, fish sauce and oil in a large mixing bowl. Toss well to coat evenly. Then, spread the pumpkin mixture on a lined baking tray.

Roast for 25 minutes in the oven, or until the pumpkin mixture is browned and cooked through. Toss once at around 15 minutes into the baking time.

Toast the shredded coconut in a dry frying pan over medium heat, tossing frequently until golden brown. Set aside to cool.

In the meantime, for the pickled red onions and chillies, mix together the vinegar and sugar in a medium-sized mixing bowl. Stir well until the sugar dissolves. Then, place the onion and chilli slices into the vinegar mixture and set aside for 10 to 15 minutes.

For the salted coconut cream, in a small mixing bowl, whisk together the coconut cream and salt until the salt dissolves. Set aside.

When ready to serve, place a dollop of salted coconut cream on a plate. Use the back of the spoon to spread it out in a circle. Place a generous serving of roasted pumpkin in the centre of the coconut cream.

Sprinkle the toasted shredded coconut over the top, followed by a few pieces of pickled red onion and chilli, then some makrut lime zest and toasted walnuts. This is best served with steamed rice or grilled flatbreads.

TIPS

» Additional root vegetables, such as carrots, potatoes, parsnips and even taro, can be used.

» Other nuts, such as cashews, peanuts or seeds, such as pumpkin and sunflower seeds, add great flavour and texture.

» The dish is vegetarian as long as the rendang paste does not contain shrimp paste.

Mum always had a heart for service and giving. My parents often went to charity fundraisers and big meetings for event planning. Sometimes they got a fancy dinner out of it and would bring my brother and me any leftover treats like little cakes or bottles of fizzy drinks. One evening, Mum returned from a fundraiser dinner with a plastic bag hanging off her wrist. It wasn't tiny slices of mud cake or lemon tarts; it was a tiny leftover portion of crab spaghetti.

"You have to try this! It's delicious!" Mum was already microwaving the container and grabbing forks.

We had only ever eaten crab in Chinese or Malaysian food. Usually it was paired with spring onion and ginger and served in its shell, but this pasta had big lumps of crabmeat sitting next to burst tomatoes and wilted basil. We tucked in. Mum was right: It was delicious. Since that night, Mum had tried to re-create the crab pasta a few times, leaving out the plasticky skinned and watery tomatoes, but always adding fish sauce and spring onions, which really gave it a boost of umami. I've twisted it even further and I think Mum would agree: My version is better.

SPICY CRAB LINGUINE

Time: 20 minutes | Makes: 4 servings

---

500 g (18 oz) uncooked linguine

4 AUS tbsp or 80 ml or ⅓ US cup + ½ tsp extra virgin olive oil

6 cloves garlic, finely sliced

1 small onion, finely diced

2 red serrano chillies, finely sliced

200 g (7 oz) cooked crab meat

½ AUS tbsp or 10 ml or 2 tsp fish sauce

½ AUS tbsp or 10 ml or 2 tsp yuzu juice

3 AUS tbsp or 13 g or 4 US tbsp finely sliced spring onion (scallion)

½ AUS cup loosely packed or 20 g or ½ US cup fresh green basil leaves

In a large pot of boiling water over medium-high heat, add 3 to 4 very generous pinches of salt. Then, add the pasta and cook, stirring occasionally, for 2 minutes less than indicated time on the packet.

While the pasta is cooking, place a large frying pan over medium-high heat. Add the oil, and once the oil is hot, sauté the garlic and onion for 1 minute, or until the garlic begins to colour. Then, add the chillies and cooked crab meat, stir-frying for another 1 minute, or until well mixed.

Drain the pasta, reserving 1 AUS cup (250 ml or 1 US cup + 2 teaspoons) of the pasta cooking water, then add the drained pasta to the frying pan. Mix thoroughly, then add the fish sauce, yuzu juice and a few AUS tablespoons (20 ml or 4 teaspoons per tablespoon) of the pasta water. Toss thoroughly to emulsify the sauce (make it creamy) and mix all the ingredients together. Add more table-spoons of water as needed to get a saucy consistency or leave it as dry as you prefer. Once mixed, turn off the heat and add the spring onion and basil leaves. Toss again to mix, then serve.

TIPS

» Halved or whole cherry tomatoes can be added just before the crab and sautéed for a minute or so to soften.

» Fresh dill and parsley are great herbs to add at the end, too.

STEAK AND "STROG" SAUCE

One weekend when I was in high school, Mum decided that Stroganoff would be a hit with the family. There were brown paper bags filled with plain old white button mushrooms, a small glass of her favourite XO Cognac and, weirdly to me, a plastic jar of thick cream. We never cooked with cream! Our food was always thickened or made creamy with corn flour (cornstarch) slurries or coconut cream. My brother and I were very excited by the prospect of thick, creamy gravy over our rice with tender beef strips and spongy mushrooms. At last, Mum finished cooking and placed a big pot of Stroganoff in front of us. We ladled the mixture eagerly over our rice, shovelled it into our mouths and started chewing . . . and chewing . . . and kept chewing! The beef was horribly tough and dry. Mum was so disappointed, but it wasn't all terrible! The sauce was amazing. The mushrooms were plump and the creamy gravy was buttery. If I recall correctly, my brother ended up eating three plates of rice smothered in "Strog sauce." This recipe borrows that amazing sauce and pairs it with deliciously tender ribeye steak.

Time: 30 minutes | Makes: 4 servings

STEAK

850 g to 1 kg (30 to 35 oz) ribeye, bone-in, at room temperature (about 2.5 cm [1"] thick or just over)

12 g (2 tsp) salt

4 g (2 tsp) coarsely ground pepper

2 AUS tbsp or 40 ml or 2 US tbsp + 2 tsp neutral oil

25 g (5 tsp) unsalted butter

2 cloves garlic, lightly crushed

4 to 5 sprigs thyme

MUSHROOM SAUCE

2 AUS tbsp or 40 ml or 2 US tbsp + 2 tsp neutral oil

1 brown onion, finely sliced

3 cloves garlic, finely minced

400 g (14 oz) Swiss brown (portobello) mushrooms, sliced thinly

2 AUS tbsp or 40 ml or 2 US tbsp + 2 tsp whisky or Cognac (optional)

1 tsp coarsely ground black pepper

50 g (3½ US tbsp) unsalted butter

½ AUS cup or 125 ml or ½ US cup + 1 tsp thick cream

1 tsp dark soy sauce

1 AUS tbsp or 20 ml or 4 tsp light soy sauce

1 AUS tbsp or 20 ml or 4 tsp mirin

For the steak, season the meat on both sides with the salt and pepper. Heat a large, heavy frying pan over high heat. Then, add the oil and swirl it around the pan to coat.

Once the oil is hot, cook the steak for 5 to 6 minutes on each side, or until cooked to your preferred doneness, adding the butter, garlic and thyme, and basting the butter and oil over the steak for the remaining 2 to 3 minutes. Then, remove the steak from the heat and transfer it to a plate. Place the garlic and thyme on top of the steak, then pour any of the butter and oil from the pan over the steak. Let the steak rest for 6 to 10 minutes. Do not wash the pan.

While the cooked steak rests, prepare the mushroom sauce: In the same frying pan the steak was cooked in, heat the oil over high heat, swirling it around the pan to coat the base. Once the oil is hot, sauté the onion and garlic for 1 to 2 minutes, or until they start to brown. Next, add the mushrooms, sautéing for another 2 to 3 minutes, or until browned and softened. Add the whisky, being careful of the flames, and stir well. Then, add the pepper and butter, stir-frying for another 1 to 2 minutes.

Pour in the cream and stir continuously until the sauce thickens and simmers. Now, stir in the dark soy sauce, light soy sauce and mirin. Stir in any resting juices from the steak. Taste and adjust the seasoning with salt, if needed.

Pour the sauce onto a serving dish. Then, slice the steak into 1-cm (⅜-inch)-thick slices. Place the steak slices and the bone on top of the sauce, garnishing with the thyme and garlic cloves.

STICKY ORANGE + SZECHUAN PEPPER CHICKEN

Crispy fried bits of chicken glazed in a bright, citrusy, sweet and sour sticky sauce is a universal favourite at any Chinese takeaway joint. It is delicious and craveable. But often, the batter is doughy, thick, undercooked in parts, the chicken tastes of bicarbonate, the sauce is sickly sweet, and after one or two bites, you've had enough. This version is an elevated, share-style homage to orange chicken or lemon chicken. The colour is vibrant, the sauce is syrupy and balanced, the chicken is tender and juicy and the Szechuan peppercorns add a beautiful floral aroma and depth of flavour. You get a little tongue tingle, too!

Time: 50 minutes | Makes: 4 servings

4 skin-on, bone-in chicken Marylands (thigh and drumstick attached) or a mix of thighs and drumsticks

12 g (2 tsp) salt

4 g (2 tsp) Chinese five-spice powder

2 AUS tbsp or 40 ml or 2 US tbsp + 2 tsp neutral oil

1 medium-sized brown onion, finely sliced

1 tsp grated fresh ginger

8 cloves garlic, minced

5 g (3 tsp) Szechuan peppercorns, toasted

2 star anise

1 cinnamon quill (stick)

2 AUS tbsp or 40 ml or 2 US tbsp + 2 tsp ABC Chilli Sauce

½ AUS cup or 125 ml or ½ US cup + 1 tsp fresh orange juice

1 medium-sized orange, finely sliced

Steamed rice, for serving

Preheat the oven to 180°C (350°F).

Place the chicken on a large tray or plate and pat the pieces dry with paper towels, then season all over with the salt and Chinese five-spice powder. Massage the salt and spices into the chicken.

Heat the oil in a large, oven-safe frying pan or skillet over medium-high heat. Cook the chicken, skin side down, until golden brown (approximately 7 to 10 minutes). Transfer the chicken to a plate, leaving any fat in the pan.

Lower the heat of the pan to medium and sauté the onion, ginger and garlic for 2 to 3 minutes. Add the Szechuan peppercorns, star anise and cinnamon quill, and cook, stirring, until fragrant, about 1 minute. Pour in the ABC Chilli Sauce and orange juice and stir until fully incorporated. Bring to a simmer.

Arrange the chicken, skin side up, in the sauce, then nestle the orange slices in and around the chicken. Transfer the pan to the oven and bake, uncovered, until the sauce is reduced and the chicken is cooked through, 30 minutes (or 20 to 25 minutes for separated thighs and drumsticks).

Transfer the chicken to a platter. Spoon the orange slices, spices and sauce over the chicken. Serve with steamed rice.

SESAME PORK BELLY
with Kimchi Sauce

My mother had a smaller fridge buzzing in the garage for all the "stinky stuff." Things like dried seafood, shrimp paste, fermented foods, garlicky things and, of course, kimchi. When the tub of kimchi would over-ferment so much that the cabbage became watery and the container would almost audibly burp every time you opened it, Mum would generally throw it out. It really wasn't until a wonderful Korean friend, Lynn, mentioned one day that over-fermented kimchi was best for stir-frying. In fact, it was perfect for kimchi fried rice! Sure enough, that week, I saved the burpy container of kimchi and made quick work of it into a delicious fried rice with pork belly and sesame oil. The short lesson in kimchi made me dive further into understanding how much potential there was in different uses of kimchi. This recipe is my way of enticing you to think differently about kimchi, pickles and other fermented foods and try them in different applications. This kimchi sauce is amazing with grilled meats, noodles, pasta, even as an alternative to Buffalo sauce for chicken wings!

Time: 40 minutes | Makes: 4 servings

PORK BELLY

750 to 800 g (26.5 to 28 oz) pork belly rashers; remove skin

6 g (2 tsp) garlic powder

1 tsp freshly ground black pepper

2 AUS tbsp or 40 ml or 2 US tbsp + 2 tsp light soy sauce

1 tsp sesame oil

1 AUS tbsp or 20 ml or 4 tsp sake

1 AUS tbsp or 20 ml or 4 tsp neutral oil

½ AUS cup or 75 g or ½ US cup + 1 tsp toasted white sesame seeds

KIMCHI SAUCE

1 AUS cup or 260 g or 1 US cup + 2 tsp cabbage kimchi

1 AUS tbsp or 20 ml or 4 tsp kimchi juice (the liquid from the kimchi)

3 AUS tbsp or 60 ml or ¼ US cup Kewpie Mayonnaise

10 ml (2 tsp) sesame oil

1 AUS tbsp or 19 g or 3½ tsp salted butter, softened

For the pork belly, in a medium-sized mixing bowl, mix together the pork belly, garlic powder, pepper, soy sauce, sesame oil, sake and neutral oil. Massage the marinade into the pork, then set aside to marinate for 10 to 15 minutes (or up to an hour), or overnight, covered, in the fridge.

In the meantime, make the kimchi sauce: Blitz all the sauce ingredients in a blender for 2 to 3 minutes on high speed until smooth. The sauce may appear frothy due to the fermentation of the kimchi.

(continued)

TIPS

» Other proteins, such as chicken, prawns (shrimp) or even beef could be used instead of pork.

» Feel free to add or replace the gai lan with your preferred vegetables.

GAI LAN

2 AUS tbsp or 40 ml or 2 US tbsp + 2 tsp neutral oil

3 cloves garlic, finely minced

340 g (12 oz) gai lan (Chinese broccoli), trimmed and cut into 5- to 7.5-cm (2" to 3") sections

2 AUS tbsp or 40 ml or 2 US tbsp + 2 tsp light soy sauce

GARNISH

Nori, sliced into thin strips

Fresh micro herbs (coriander [cilantro], shiso, tatsoi, mizuna)

Next, for the gai lan, to a large frying pan or wok over high heat, add the neutral oil. Once the oil is hot, add the garlic and gai lan. Stir-fry for 2 minutes, then add the light soy sauce. Stir-fry again for another 2 to 3 minutes, or until the stems of the gai lan are al dente. Remove from the heat.

Pan-fry the pork belly over medium heat for 4 to 5 minutes each side. Once cooked through, dip both sides of each pork belly rasher into a plate of toasted sesame seeds to coat.

Spoon a generous amount of the kimchi sauce onto a serving dish. Place the sautéed gai lan on top of the sauce, followed by the crusted pork belly. Garnish with nori strips and micro herbs.

Just as Italians meld anchovies into their sauces to boost the savouriness, the umami, the depth of flavour, Mum was always looking for ways to inject more deliciousness into her food. When my brother and I asked for spaghetti and meatballs for the first time, probably after seeing it on an American sitcom on the telly, Mum's response was to shake a drizzle of fish sauce into the pork mixture and drop a spoonful of miso into the bubbling tomato sauce. Though you can taste hints of the miso every now and again, you really wouldn't be able to "name that flavour" unless you knew it had been added.

SPAGHETTI + MEATBALLS-ISH

Mum's meatballs were definitely a lot crumblier and drier the first time she made them. Since then, I've learnt to add breadcrumbs or panko, Parmigiano-Reggiano, onion, egg and use a higher fat percentage of pork. These ingredients help create more tender, juicy meatballs.

Time: 30 minutes | Makes: 4 servings

SPAGHETTI AND MEATBALLS

1 large brown onion

4 cloves garlic, finely minced

500 g (17.5 oz) pork mince (ground pork, minimum 20% fat)

1 large egg

½ AUS cup or 31 g or ½ US cup + 1 tsp panko

¼ AUS cup or 16 g or ¼ US cup + ½ tsp fresh parsley, finely chopped

¼ AUS cup or 26 g or ¼ US cup + ½ tsp freshly grated Parmigiano-Reggiano

½ tsp salt, plus more if needed

1 AUS tbsp or 20 ml or 4 tsp fish sauce

1 tsp freshly ground black pepper

2 AUS tbsp or 40 ml or 2 US tbsp + 2 tsp olive oil

500 g (18 oz) uncooked spaghetti

Begin with the meatballs. In a food processor, blitz the onion and garlic until coarsely puréed. Alternatively, use a box grater to grate the onion and finely mince the garlic. Transfer to a large mixing bowl.

Add the pork mince, egg, panko, parsley, Parmigiano-Reggiano, ½ teaspoon of salt, fish sauce and black pepper. Use your hands to mix vigorously until all the ingredients are fully incorporated. This will take approximately 2 to 3 minutes of consistent mixing and kneading. The mixture should be uniform and the mince should appear tacky and blended, not crumbly.

Take a heaped AUS tablespoon (about 25 g or 1 US tablespoon + 2 teaspoons) of the meatball mixture and roll it into a tight ball. Repeat with all the mince.

Heat the olive oil in a large, non-stick frying pan over medium-high heat. Once hot, add the meatballs and cook for 3 to 4 minutes, rotating them occasionally to brown all over.

While the meatballs cook, bring a large pot of water to a boil over medium-high heat. Add two large pinches of salt to the boiling water, stir it, then add the spaghetti. Cook for 6 to 7 minutes. Do not drain. While the spaghetti is cooking, remove the cooked meatballs from the pan and set aside.

(continued)

TIP

» The more you work the mince by kneading it, the more bouncy or tough the meatball will be. But if you don't knead and mix the mince enough, the mixture will be uneven and crumblier.

SAUCE

4 AUS tbsp or 80 ml or ⅓ US cup olive oil

1 small onion (brown, white or yellow)

4 cloves garlic, minced

10 ml (2 tsp) miso (red or white)

2 AUS tbsp or 40 ml or 2 US tbsp + 2 tsp tomato paste

800 g (28 oz) canned whole peeled Italian tomatoes

¼ AUS cup or 16 g or ¼ US cup + ½ tsp chopped fresh parsley

Fish sauce (optional)

SERVING

Fresh red or green serrano chillies, thinly sliced

Fresh green basil, torn

Fresh parsley, finely chopped

Parmigiano-Reggiano

Next, prepare the sauce. Add the olive oil to the pan the meatballs had been cooked in, still over medium-high heat. Once hot, sauté the onion and garlic for 2 to 3 minutes, or until beginning to brown. Next, add the miso and tomato paste. Sauté for a further 2 to 3 minutes. Then, add the tomatoes and parsley, using a spatula or spoon to chop or squash them roughly. Stir well to incorporate.

Place the meatballs into the sauce. Then, using tongs or a spaghetti fork/server, transfer the spaghetti directly from the cooking water into the sauce, along with about ½ AUS cup (125 ml or ½ US cup + 1 teaspoon) of the pasta water. Stir and toss the pasta and meatballs together to emulsify and mix the sauce thoroughly. Once combined, taste for seasoning. If more salt is needed, season with fish sauce (if using) or salt.

Serve the pasta with extra chillies, basil, parsley and grated Parmigiano-Reggiano.

CUMIN LAMB RIBS

with Green Sauce

This is one of those special occasion recipes. Lamb ribs are notoriously rich, full of gamey flavour and luxurious belly fat. You need something herbaceous and sour to cut through the richness and achieve that lip-smacking deliciousness. The added layer of bittersweetness from the cumin creates a really unique and aromatic experience. With any fattier cut of meat that you are roasting, adding water to the bottom of the roasting tray creates steam which surrounds the meat and helps the fat render out. It also prevents the meat from drying out.

Time: 2 hours 30 minutes | Makes: 4 servings

MARINADE

6 cloves garlic, finely minced

1 AUS tbsp or 9 g or 4 tsp ground cumin

1 AUS tbsp or 8 g or 1 US tbsp + 1 tsp ground coriander seeds

1 tsp freshly ground black pepper

1 AUS tbsp or 20 ml or 4 tsp fish sauce

1½ AUS tbsp or 30 ml or 2 US tbsp light soy sauce

1 AUS tbsp or 20 ml or 4 tsp neutral oil

1.4 kg (3 lb) lamb rib racks, trimmed

SERVING

Green Sauce (page 19)

Lemon wedges

Preheat the oven to 150°C (300°F). Mix together all the ingredients for the marinade. Rub both sides of the lamb ribs with the marinade.

Place the lamb ribs on a rack over a roasting tray. Pour 2 cm (¾ inch) of boiling water into the tray. Carefully place the lamb and tray in the oven and roast for 2½ hours, or until fork-tender. Then, remove the ribs from the oven and allow to rest for 15 to 20 minutes.

Slice the ribs between the bones and stack the individual ribs high on a serving platter. Pour any of the resting juices over them, then dollop green sauce over the ribs and serve with wedges of lemon.

TIPS

» You can marinate the lamb ribs for up to 48 hours before cooking.

» This recipe would also work with lamb riblets (individual ribs). The roasting time can be reduced from 2½ hours to 1½ hours.

» Lamb may be replaced with pork.

PAPPARDELLE

with Rosemary +
Five-Spice Duck

There are a couple of must-haves on the Christmas feast table. One of them is a whole roast duck seasoned generously with Chinese five-spice powder, soy sauce and pepper. It comes out of the oven beautifully mahogany brown and it smells of cloves and star anise and fennel seed. It is a pure joy to roast and to serve, but don't worry; this recipe won't require you to roast a whole duck. Usually there are leftovers, as with most of the bigger dishes on Christmas. I concocted this recipe initially with truffle oil, but it was rich and heavy and we ended up with even more leftovers. What it needed was a zing, a pop, a little something to tickle the taste buds and make the family want to eat the whole dish. That's where the tamarind sauce comes in. Surprisingly, the Asian ingredients of five-spice and tamarind go beautifully with rosemary. It's a characteristically Christmassy aroma and flavour. I do recommend using pappardelle or a wide-shaped pasta like paccheri. The broad shape gets coated in sauce and has enough body to match the heavy duck.

Time: 2 hours | Makes: 4 servings

2 duck legs (drumsticks and thighs)

1 AUS tbsp or 8 g or 4 tsp Chinese five-spice powder

1 AUS tbsp or 20 ml or 4 tsp light soy sauce

1 tsp coarsely ground black pepper

10 ml (2 tsp) neutral oil

320 g (11.5 oz) dried egg pappardelle

2 AUS tbsp or 38 g or 2½ US tbsp salted butter

10 ml (2 tsp) olive oil

4 cloves garlic, finely minced

2 AUS tbsp or 5 g or 2 US tbsp + 2 tsp fresh rosemary leaves, finely chopped

Sweet + Sour Tamarind Sauce (page 20), for serving

Preheat the oven to 180°C (350°F).

Pat the duck legs dry with paper towel and lightly score or poke the skin with a sharp knife to create slits for the fat to render out.

In a small bowl, mix together the five-spice powder, soy sauce, pepper and neutral oil until you have a thick marinade. Coat both duck legs with the marinade and transfer them to a lined roasting tray. Roast for 75 minutes. Then, transfer the duck legs to a plate or dish and allow them to rest for 30 minutes. Once rested, shred the duck meat, reserving any resting juices.

Bring a large pot of water to a boil over medium-high heat. Once boiling, add a few generous pinches of salt. Then, add the pappardelle and cook until al dente (approximately 6 to 7 minutes).

While the pasta is boiling, place a large frying pan over medium-high heat. Once hot, add the butter and olive oil. Add the garlic and rosemary and fry for about 1 minute, or until fragrant and the garlic is beginning to colour. Then, using tongs or a spaghetti fork/server, transfer the pappardelle directly from the cooking water into the hot butter and rosemary mixture. Add 5 to 6 AUS tablespoons (100 to 120 ml or 7 to 9 US tablespoons) of the pasta water, along with the shredded duck and any resting juices. Toss the pappardelle very well to combine.

Serve with a drizzle of Sweet + Sour Tamarind Sauce.

TIPS

» This recipe would work with store-bought pre-cooked duck or leftover roast duck.

» Alternatively, try this with lamb or other gamey proteins.

Sunday church services were always followed by a huge pot-luck lunch where members of the congregation brought dishes in to share. My mother and I often spent hours on the Saturday night before, preparing and cooking batches of stews, noodles, pastries and braised dishes. My mother always had a heart of generosity and servitude; I think she immersed herself in church out of comfort. It wasn't long before I started to feel obligated to help her. My heart was firmly rooted in serving my mother rather than the church, so I was mostly happy to spend hours stirring, chopping and packing alongside her.

The wonderful smorgasbord was always buzzing with liveliness and a wonderful variety of aromas. There were dishes from so many different cuisines. One particular dish that I always looked forward to was a Sri Lankan dish with plump, juicy portions of white fish bathed in the bright yellow, aromatic sauce. "*Meen kulambu!*" the gentle, doe-eyed woman behind the dish would say. Oh, it was succulent and full of savoury and sour notes. Kulambu is a tangy broth or sauce often described as a "curry." I detest the word *curry*. I find it generic and lazy when it comes to describing South Asian cuisine. In fact, South Asians didn't adopt that word until colonisation. I encourage you to state this dish's name as it rings true when you make this: meen kulambu. It is as love-filled, journeyed and stomach-warming as the gentle old soul that introduced it to me.

SRI LANKAN FISH IN SPICY COCONUT SAUCE

(Meen Kulambu)

Time: 40 minutes | Makes: 4 servings

MEEN KULAMBU PASTE

4 AUS tbsp or 80 ml or ⅓ US cup oil

1 large brown onion, diced

4 cloves garlic, finely chopped

3 slices fresh ginger

10 dried red chillies, rehydrated in 1 AUS cup or 250 ml or 1 US cup + 2 tsp hot water for 15 minutes, divided

1 tsp cumin seeds

½ tsp freshly ground black pepper

1 AUS tbsp or 8 g or 4 tsp ground coriander seeds

1 tsp ground turmeric

1 tsp fenugreek

2 large red tomatoes, diced

2 AUS tbsp or 40 ml or 2 US tbsp + 2 tsp tomato paste

½ AUS cup or 125 ml or ½ US cup + 1 tsp Sweet + Sour Tamarind Sauce (page 20)

12 g (2 tsp) salt

Starting with the meen kulambu paste, heat the oil over medium-high heat, then stir-fry the onion, garlic, ginger and about six of the rehydrated red chillies, reserving the liquid for later use. Once the onion starts to brown, add the cumin, black pepper, coriander, turmeric and fenugreek. Stir-fry for 1 to 2 minutes, or until fragrant.

Next, add the tomatoes, stir-frying again for 1 to 2 minutes. Then, add the tomato paste, Sweet + Sour Tamarind Sauce and ½ AUS cup (125 ml or ½ US cup + 1 teaspoon) of the chilli soaking water and the salt, reserving the remaining four rehydrated red chillies for the next step. Cook for 3 to 4 minutes, or until the tomatoes are very soft. Transfer everything to a blender and blitz until smooth.

(continued)

STIR-FRIED AROMATICS

3 AUS tbsp or 60 ml or ¼ US cup oil

1 large brown onion, diced

4 cloves garlic, finely chopped

15 curry leaves

4 g (2 tsp) cumin seeds

4 g (2 tsp) fennel seeds

4 g (2 tsp) ground turmeric

1 AUS tbsp or 8 g or 4 tsp jaggery or palm sugar

1 AUS cup or 250 ml or 1 US cup + 2 tsp coconut milk

675 g (1½ lb) ling fish or cod fillets

Salt

SERVING

Green serrano or jalapeño chilli, finely sliced

Fresh tomato, finely diced

Cooked basmati rice

For the stir-fried aromatics, in a large frying pan, wok or saucepan, heat the oil over medium-high heat. Sauté the onion, garlic, remaining four rehydrated red chillies and curry leaves for 2 to 3 minutes, or until the onion begins to brown. Then, add the cumin and fennel seeds, turmeric and jaggery, and sauté for a further 1 to 2 minutes.

Now, pour in the meen kulambu paste. Stir thoroughly, then add the coconut milk. Stir thoroughly again and bring to a simmer. Lower the heat to medium, then add the fish. Coat the fish in the sauce, then let simmer gently for 4 to 5 minutes. Season to taste with salt. Then, turn off the heat.

Serve garnished with the sliced green chilli and tomato along with the rice.

TIPS

» Ling can be replaced with any firm white fish or prawns (shrimp).

» The Sweet + Sour Tamarind Sauce can be replaced with equal parts tamarind purée and tomato paste for a hacked version.

GARLICKY SEAFOOD CLAYPOT RICE

In Malaysia, when you go to a claypot restaurant, you're met with rows and rows of claypots almost set ablaze on a row of burners. The aroma of rice, sauce and various toppings like sweet Chinese sausage, pork ribs and chicken fills the restaurant. The sauce is a little sweet, salty and always quite simple. It is a special sight! The best claypots are the ones with squid, mussels and prawns in them. So, you can imagine when I was devising this recipe, I went hard on all those best bits. This is an absolute treat to eat, and when it lands on the table, it is spectacular.

Time: 40 minutes | Makes: 4 servings

3 AUS cups or 609 g or 3 US cups + 4 tsp uncooked rice, rinsed well and drained

3 AUS cups or 750 ml or 3 US cups + 2 US tbsp chicken stock

1 AUS tbsp or 20 ml or 4 tsp oyster sauce

2 AUS tbsp or 40 ml or 2 US tbsp + 2 tsp fish sauce

½ AUS tbsp or 10 g or 4 tsp grated fresh ginger

10 cloves garlic, minced, divided

32 g (1 oz) lap cheong (Chinese sausage)

100 g (3.5 oz) squid or calamari, sliced into small pieces

100 g (3.5 oz) prawns (shrimp), deshelled + deveined

100 g (3.5 oz) mussel meat

100 g (3.5 oz) baby octopus

1 tsp freshly ground black pepper

2 AUS tbsp or 40 ml or 2 US tbsp + 2 tsp mirin

1 AUS tbsp or 20 ml or 4 tsp light soy sauce

1 AUS tbsp or 20 ml or 4 tsp fish sauce

½ AUS cup or 125 ml or ½ US cup + 1 tsp Green Sauce (page 19), for serving

Place the rinsed and drained rice in a large claypot, wok, casserole dish, saucepan or high-sided, heavy-based frying pan on the stove. Then, pour in the chicken stock, oyster sauce and fish sauce, and add the ginger and half of the garlic. Stir well, then place the lid on the pot. Steam over medium heat for 20 minutes, or until the rice has just cooked through.

In the meantime, in a medium-sized mixing bowl, combine the lap cheong, squid, prawns, mussels, octopus, remaining garlic, pepper, mirin, soy sauce and fish sauce. Mix well.

When the rice has just cooked through, increase the heat to high, remove the lid from the pot and spread the seafood mixture and any excess sauce over the rice. Place the lid back on and continue to cook for 6 to 8 minutes, or until the seafood is just cooked through. Remove from the heat.

This step is optional, but if inclined, use a food-safe blow torch on the top of the seafood to add smoky flavour and some char.

Serve the pot on the centre of the table along with Green Sauce (see Tips).

TIPS

» If you haven't made the Green Sauce (page 19) to use in this recipe, feel free to use a mixture of your favourite fresh herbs and adjust the seasoning as you like.

» Try adding pork mince (ground pork) or sliced chicken thighs before the seafood.

» If you would like the rice to be crispier on the base, leave the pot on the stove for an extra few minutes, with the lid off.

ROASTED CAULIFLOWER

with Macadamia + Miso Butter

Roasted cauliflower became viral over the last four or five years. It's on every menu at every casual dining and semi-fine dining restaurant I can think of. There's a totally good reason for it: It's damn delicious. A lot of people think that cauliflower has a gassy or "farty" smell. That only happens when it is over-cooked. When cooked right, it has a prominent sweetness, a gentle creaminess and nuttiness. These characteristics make it ideal to be paired with salty, nutty, full-bodied macadamia and miso butter. This impressive dish is very easy to make and satisfies vegetarians and non-vegetarians alike. This is a go-to recipe for dinner parties and long weekend lunches.

Time: 35 minutes | Makes: 4 servings

CAULIFLOWER

½ AUS cup or 125 ml or ½ US cup + 1 tsp mirin

1 AUS tbsp or 24 g or 4 tsp salt

½ large cauliflower, cut into 2 or 3 wedges

MACADAMIA AND MISO BUTTER

2 AUS tbsp or 40 ml or 2 US tbsp + 2 tsp neutral oil, divided

4 cloves garlic, finely chopped

90 g (⅔ US cup) macadamias, very roughly chopped

100 g (7 US tbsp) unsalted butter

1 AUS tbsp or 21 g or 4 tsp white miso (shiro miso)

½ AUS cup or 125 ml or ½ US cup + 1 tsp water

Juice of 1 lemon

GARNISH

Finely sliced shiso (perilla)

Bring 1 litre (1 quart) of water to a boil in a large saucepan over medium-high heat. Add the mirin, salt and cauliflower wedges. Boil for 4 to 5 minutes. Then, remove from the heat and drain the cauliflower well. Allow to steam dry on a tray or rack until cool (approximately 10 minutes).

In a large frying pan over medium-high heat, add 1 AUS tablespoon (20 ml or 4 teaspoons) of neutral oil. When the oil is hot, place the cauliflower wedges in the pan on one of the flat-cut faces. Allow to fry and char undisturbed for 5 to 6 minutes. Flip the cauliflower wedges onto the other flat sides and fry again for 5 to 6 minutes. Then, flip the cauliflower onto the curved sides and fry undisturbed for 2 to 3 minutes, or until well browned. Remove the cauliflower from the heat and lower the heat on the pan to medium.

Add the remaining AUS tablespoon (20 ml or 4 teaspoons) of neutral oil, garlic and macadamias to the hot pan. Stir-fry until the garlic and macadamias begin to colour. Then, add the butter. Swirl the pan around, and once the butter is melted and becomes foamy, add the miso and water. Stir thoroughly to dissolve the miso completely. Turn off the heat and add the lemon juice.

Plate the cauliflower wedges in a dish, then pour the macadamia and miso butter over the cauliflower. Garnish with finely sliced shiso.

TIPS

» If the sauce is too thick, add a few AUS tablespoons (20 ml or 4 teaspoons per tablespoon) of water to thin it out. Adjust the seasoning with salt and more lemon juice.

» This recipe works with other hardy vegetables like broccoli, pumpkin, potatoes and carrots.

CHARRED CABBAGE

with Coriander, Curry Leaf Pesto and Cashew Cream

Similar to the Roasted Cauliflower recipe on page 64, roasted wedges of cabbage became extremely popular in the last few years for good reason. Cabbages and cauliflower belong to the same family as broccoli: brassicas. The vegetables in this family really benefit from charring. Blackening and caramelising the vegetables draws out natural sweetness and adds a bitter note that complements the caramelised sugars. Forget boiling or steaming your brassicas. Char them, burn them lightly, barbecue them, smoke them, get enough colour on them and they have the potential to be the most delicious vegetable dishes you make. The curry leaf pesto is a huge hit of flavour that has quickly become a favourite at barbecues for my friends and it's brilliant with skewered meat, grilled steaks, barbecue chicken and grilled mushrooms.

Time: 1 hour | Makes: 4 servings

CHARRED CABBAGE

1 AUS tbsp or 20 ml or 4 tsp neutral oil

1 tsp salt

1 tsp freshly ground black pepper

¼ large cabbage, divided into 2 wedges

CASHEW CREAM

2 AUS cups or 500 ml or 2 US cups + 2 US tbsp full-fat milk

⅔ AUS cup or 97 g or ⅔ US cup + 1 US tbsp toasted cashew nuts

½ tsp salt

CURRY LEAF PESTO

½ AUS cup or 10 g or 0.5 oz fresh curry leaves, finely chopped

4 roots' worth fresh coriander (cilantro), finely chopped

4 cloves garlic, finely minced

½ AUS cup or 73 g or ½ US cup + 1 US tbsp toasted cashew nuts, finely chopped

1 tsp caster (superfine) sugar

2 AUS tbsp or 40 ml or 2 US tbsp + 2 tsp fish sauce

1 AUS tbsp or 20 ml or 4 tsp white vinegar

2 AUS tbsp or 40 ml or 2 US tbsp + 2 tsp neutral oil

Preheat the oven to 180°C (350°F).

For the charred cabbage, in a small bowl, whisk together the neutral oil, salt and pepper, then drizzle this mixture over the wedges of cabbage. Use your hands to massage the oil and seasoning into the cabbage.

Place a medium-sized frying pan over medium heat. Place the cabbage in the pan and fry undisturbed for 5 to 6 minutes each side, or until charred. Then, place the cabbage in an oven-safe dish, or transfer the whole frying pan if oven-safe, to the oven to roast for 10 minutes.

In the meantime, for the cashew cream, place the milk, cashew nuts and salt in a small saucepan over medium heat and bring to a boil for 10 to 15 minutes, or until the milk has reduced by half. Transfer the hot mixture to a blender and blitz until smooth. Set aside.

For the curry leaf pesto, make sure the curry leaves, coriander, garlic and cashew nuts are very finely chopped, then combine them with the sugar, fish sauce, vinegar and oil in a bowl and mix thoroughly. Taste and adjust the seasoning.

To serve, place a large dollop of cashew cream on a dish. Place the cabbage on top of the cream, then drizzle the curry leaf pesto generously over the top.

TIPS

» If you use smaller wedges of cabbage, you may not need to roast them in the oven for 10 minutes. The charring may cook the cabbage all the way through. Use a fork or knife to test the tenderness of the cabbage. There should be little resistance.

» Instead of plain white vinegar, try using fresh lemon or lime juice in the pesto for an added flavour.

» Alternative nuts to use include walnuts, almonds or macadamias.

SOMETHING LIGHT

I want these dishes the most on warm evenings with a sticky humidity hanging in the air, cicadas ringing through the trees, bare feet propped up on the outdoor dining chairs and friends and family popping open another bottle of wine. Alternatively, if I had to come up with a menu for date night, I'd pick things out of this chapter. You'll find these dishes are herbaceous, acidic celebrations of flavour-bomb morsels perfect for sharing. I think the most effective way to use this chapter is to pick any combination of these recipes and serve them all as a beautiful, light spread for a long leisurely lunch or dinner party.

These aren't modernised versions of food Mum made, but they adopt her curiosity of unusual flavour combinations and textures. This chapter arises from years of exploration, experimentation and learning about food from other cultures. Travelling unlocked a reverence and emotional connection to the different ways I saw people cook, eat and use the land around them. Everything I saw, smelled, tasted, touched had a huge impact on the way I approached flavours and ingredients.

Sadly, I wasn't able to share these recipes with Mum. In a way, this chapter is an offering of thanks to her for showing me how to impart my own emotion and care for others into my food.

WATERMELON SALAD

with Tamarind Salmon Floss

This recipe is inspired by my friend Chef Bee Satongun. She is chef-owner of Michelin-starred Thai restaurant Paste in Bangkok and its little sister, Paste Australia in a tiny town south of Sydney called Mittagong. Chef Bee was also awarded the title of Asia's Best Female Chef by World's 50 Best Restaurants in 2018. But accolades aside, Chef Bee is warm and full of life, with a laser focus and pride in her work. My mother would have loved Chef Bee and her innovative, flavoursome food. On Chef Bee's menu, there is a dish of watermelon, salmon floss, roasted galangal, shallots and trout caviar. "Flossing" meat like chicken, pork or fish is very common in Asian cuisine. It's something I grew up eating often in a sandwich, on eggs or just as a snack out of a bag. Chef Bee's watermelon salad challenged my expectations of the flavours and presentation of modern Thai food. My version adds a few more textures and uses bold, fragrant flavours I love, like basil and tamarind.

Time: 1 hour | Makes: 4 servings

3 AUS cups or 469 g or 3 US cups + 2 US tbsp fresh seedless watermelon cubes (1.5-cm [½"] cubes), rind reserved

2 Lebanese cucumbers, peeled, deseeded and finely diced

½ AUS cup or 125 ml or ½ US cup + 1 tsp white vinegar

9 g (2 tsp) sugar

12 g (2 tsp) salt

SALMON FLOSS

300 g (10.5 oz) skinless, boneless salmon fillet

1 tsp freshly ground black pepper

1 AUS tbsp or 20 ml or 4 tsp neutral oil

½ AUS tbsp or 10 ml or 2 tsp light soy sauce

3 AUS tbsp or 60 ml or ¼ US cup Sweet + Sour Tamarind Sauce (page 20)

SERVING

Fresh basil leaves

Finger limes (optional; grapefruit or pomelo can be used)

Salmon or trout roe (optional)

Keep the watermelon and cucumber cubes in the fridge to chill. Taking the reserved watermelon rind, make thin slices of the white part, discarding the hard outer green parts.

Finely shred the strips of white rind with a knife and mix together with the vinegar, sugar and salt. Place in the fridge to pickle while preparing the salmon floss.

Pat the salmon fillet dry with paper towels, then season liberally with pepper. Place a small, non-stick frying pan over medium heat and add the oil. Once the oil is hot, place the salmon fillet in the pan and fry for 3 to 4 minutes each side. Then, use a spatula or wooden spoon to break up the salmon into very small pieces. Continue to stir-fry and break up the salmon for another 5 to 10 minutes, or until crumbly.

Then, lower the heat to low and add the soy sauce and Sweet + Sour Tamarind Sauce. Continue to break up the salmon pieces with a fork or spatula frequently as they cook for another 20 to 30 minutes, or until flossy and crisped up. Set aside to cool.

To serve, portion out a mixture of watermelon and cucumber in each bowl, then some drained pickled rind, a generous sprinkle of salmon floss and garnish with basil, finger limes and salmon roe.

TIPS

» If the salmon does not appear flossed but comes up crumbly or hard, simply pulse it in a food processor until the desired floss consistency.

» Salmon or pork floss can be used and purchased from Asian supermarkets or specialty stores.

TOM YUM CEVICHE

My mother and I shared a love of four food categories: sour, spicy, soupy, seafoody. These favourite elements come together in a classic *tom yum*. My mother also loved ceviche, introduced to her by one of her Peruvian patients. When I think of ceviche, I think of citrus, superb-quality fish, a little spice, lots of herbs, things that definitely cross over with our favourite elements of Southeast Asian cuisine. This tom yum ceviche brings the best of both worlds in a very elegant fashion. The flavours are exciting and the textures in this dish are dynamic; the consistency of the fish literally transforms in front of you as the acidity in the dressing cooks the fish the longer it sits in it.

Time: 15 minutes | Makes: 4 servings

300 g (10.5 oz) sashimi-grade kingfish, sliced into 5-mm (scant ¼") slices

DRESSING

4 to 5 sprigs coriander (cilantro), stems very finely sliced, leaves removed and reserved

1 AUS tbsp or 20 ml or 4 tsp tom yum paste

Juice of 2 limes

¼ AUS cup or 63 ml or ¼ US cup + ½ tsp coconut water

1 AUS tbsp or 20 ml or 4 tsp fish sauce

SERVING

8 to 10 cherry tomatoes, quartered

2 red serrano chillies, deseeded, finely sliced

2 lemongrass stalks (white part only), very finely sliced

6 makrut lime leaves, very finely shredded (less than 1 mm [1/32"] thick)

Arrange the slices of kingfish on a platter and set aside in the fridge until ready to serve.

Next, in a medium-sized mixing bowl, combine all the dressing ingredients. Stir thoroughly until the tom yum paste is fully incorporated. Taste and adjust the seasoning. The dressing should be particularly sour so it cooks the fish over time. Set the dressing aside in the fridge until ready to serve.

When ready to serve, scatter the tomatoes and chillies on top of the kingfish. Then, pour just enough of the dressing over the kingfish so that each piece of fish has been lightly coated. Pour any remaining dressing into a serving dish for guests to add extra as they please.

Scatter the lemongrass and makrut lime leaves over the kingfish and tomatoes. Then, garnish with the reserved coriander leaves. Serve while still cold.

TIPS

» This ceviche can be made with fresh, sashimi-grade prawns (shrimp), scallops and other fish.

» Always taste the dressing before adding it to the fish. The dressing should be just slightly saltier, sweeter and sourer than your ideal balance as you want stronger flavours to be able to permeate the fish and other ingredients.

SMOKED EGGPLANT
with Peanut Dressing

Since watching an elderly Lebanese man blister and char eggplants whole on the gas stove as I waited for my doner kebab (gyro) one afternoon in my early twenties, I have been obsessed with cooking eggplants this way. The smoky, charry, buttery sweetness of the eggplant is the true secret to the best eggplant dips, salads and general dishes. The peanut dressing is addictive and garlic heavy and contains caraway seeds, a highly under-used spice with mild peppery liquorice vibes. The fish sauce is what adds a savoury, lip-smacking quality to the dressing. This dish is a great start to a meal or player in a spread of dishes; full of satisfying toasty flavour.

Time: 30 to 40 minutes | Makes: 4 servings

2 large globe eggplants

PEANUT DRESSING

1 AUS cup or 250 ml or 1 US cup + 2 tsp neutral oil

½ AUS cup or 76 g or ½ US cup + ½ US tbsp unsalted peanuts, roughly chopped

6 cloves garlic, peeled and lightly crushed

1 star anise

3.5 g (2 tsp) coriander seeds

4 g (2 tsp) caraway seeds

4 g (2 tsp) cumin seeds

1 AUS tbsp or 11 g or 4 tsp toasted sesame seeds

6 dried chiles de arbol, roughly chopped into 1.5-cm (½") pieces

5 g (2 tsp) ground smoked paprika

1 AUS tbsp or 20 ml or 4 tsp fish sauce

SERVING

Lemon juice and zest

Fresh parsley leaves

Crusty bread

Place a wire rack over a large gas hob (burner), and place the two eggplants on the rack. Turn the heat of the hob to high and char the eggplants all over, rotating occasionally. This process can take anywhere between 10 and 20 minutes. Once the eggplants are blackened and soft, place them in a large mixing bowl and cover with cling film (plastic wrap). Set aside for 10 minutes.

In the meantime, start the peanut dressing. Heat the oil in a small saucepan over medium heat. Once hot, add the peanuts and fry until lightly golden. Remove the peanuts from the oil with a slotted spoon and drain on paper towels.

Lower the heat to low, then add the garlic, star anise, coriander seeds, caraway seeds and cumin seeds. Fry for 5 to 8 minutes, or until the garlic is deep golden brown and the oil is fragrant.

In the meantime, place the drained peanuts, sesame seeds, chiles de arbol, paprika and fish sauce in a medium-sized mixing bowl or a Mason jar. Turn the heat beneath the saucepan back to medium for 1 minute, then very carefully pour the hot oil mixture into the mixing bowl or jar. Leave to steep uncovered for 10 to 15 minutes, or until cool to touch. Then stir thoroughly.

Peel the skin off the eggplants, trying to keep the eggplant as intact as you can. Remove the stem. Then, slice the eggplant into thick strips and lay them in a dish. Stir the peanut dressing thoroughly again and spoon the chunky bits with some oil over the eggplant. Garnish with a squeeze of fresh lemon, some lemon zest and the parsley leaves. Serve with crusty bread.

SPICY SALMON TARTARE

My mother and brother share a love of salmon sashimi. They love the fatty, meaty, almost creamy richness of high-quality salmon. For me, it's second to tuna. However, understanding the way fat can help carry flavour and affect the way ingredients feel in the mouth became a vital lesson for me to learn as I started cooking professionally. My food is textural food, with everything serving a purpose and impacting taste. The spice and crunch of Lao Gan Ma Crispy Chilli Oil with the fatty salmon and creamy coconut adds layers of richness, which is cut by the sweet and sour pickled shallots and almost smoky curry leaves. Then the flavour is rounded again with fried peanuts, offering another form of savouriness in a crunchy texture. This is a very easy dish that I consistently make for dinner parties and is one of the most popular light courses on my catering menu.

Time: 20 to 25 minutes | Makes: 4 servings

PICKLED SHALLOTS

9 g (2 tsp) caster (superfine) sugar

½ AUS cup or 125 ml or ½ US cup + 1 tsp white vinegar

2 red Asian shallots, finely sliced

SALMON TARTARE

300g (10.5 oz) sashimi-grade salmon, cut into 6-mm (¼") cubes

2 AUS tbsp or 40 ml or 2 US tbsp + 2 tsp Lao Gan Ma Crispy Chilli Oil

1 AUS tbsp or 20 ml or 4 tsp fish sauce

TOPPING

Neutral oil, for frying

20 to 30 curry leaves

⅓ AUS cup or 50 g or ⅓ US cup + ½ tsp unsalted peanuts

SERVING

1 AUS cup or 250 ml or 1 US cup + 2 tsp full-fat coconut cream

4 g (⅔ tsp) salt

Lettuce cups (optional)

Sliced cucumber (optional)

Prawn (shrimp) crackers (optional)

Crackers (optional)

For the pickled shallots, in a medium-sized mixing bowl, dissolve the sugar in the vinegar. Then, add the shallots and mix well. Set aside for 10 to 15 minutes.

For the salmon tartare, in a medium-sized mixing bowl, combine the salmon, Lao Gan Ma Crispy Chilli Oil and fish sauce. Mix thoroughly and set aside in the fridge.

For the topping, to a small frying pan over medium heat, add just 1.5 cm (½ inch) of oil. Once hot, carefully add the curry leaves and beware of their popping. Once the curry leaves have crisped up and become translucent (approximately 10 to 15 seconds), remove them from the oil and drain on paper towels.

With the oil still over medium heat, add the peanuts and fry for 3 to 4 minutes, or until browned. Remove the peanuts from the oil and drain on paper towels. Leave the peanuts to cool and crisp up.

In the meantime, mix together the coconut cream and salt in a small mixing bowl until the salt has dissolved.

Once the peanuts have cooled and become crunchy, roughly chop them. Add two-thirds of the peanuts and drained pickled shallots to the salmon mixture and stir thoroughly to mix well.

Spread the coconut cream mixture on a serving dish, followed by the salmon tartare. Then, garnish with the remaining fried peanuts and the crispy curry leaves. Serve the tartare on its own or with lettuce cups, sliced cucumber, prawn crackers or other crackers.

TIPS

» Other fish can be used in this recipe. I recommend a fattier fish, like kingfish, that will stand up to the richness of the dressing.

» This can also be made with chilled, poached or grilled chicken.

TUNA CRUDO, NASHI PEAR, DAIKON, PONZU AND WASABI CREAM

I adore raw tuna. I love all grades of fattiness of tuna (*akami, chutoro, toro, otoro*). To me, it is superior to salmon and much cleaner in flavour. This means it can carry extremes of flavours like sweetness, bitterness, or saltiness far better than richness. There is nothing worse to me than beautiful tuna smothered in mayonnaise or cheese. But that being said, a little bit of fattiness from a small amount of mayonnaise or egg yolk can really play well. In this recipe, I have opted to balance sweetness and bitterness by using sweet and crisp Nashi pears, sharp and bitter daikon and ponzu. A splash of yuzu aroma plays well with the citrus in the ponzu, which, along with the bitter and hot wasabi, is tempered by a dollop of mayonnaise and the fatty creaminess of avocado.

Time: 15 to 20 minutes | Makes: 4 servings

300 g (10.5 oz) sushi-grade tuna loin, thinly sliced

WASABI CREAM

¼ AUS cup or 63 ml or ¼ US cup + ½ tsp Kewpie Mayonnaise (or other Japanese mayonnaise)

½ avocado, peeled and pitted

6.5 g (2 tsp) wasabi

Salt (optional)

ASSEMBLY

Juice of ½ lemon

1 Nashi pear

½ AUS cup or 115 g or ½ US cup + 1 tsp grated fresh daikon (excess moisture squeezed out)

2 to 3 AUS tbsp or 40 to 60 ml or 2½ to 4 US tbsp Ponzu (page 24)

SERVING

1 tsp toasted white sesame seeds

Cress or shiso leaves

Place the sliced tuna in the fridge to chill.

Prepare the wasabi cream by placing the mayonnaise, avocado and wasabi in a blender and blending until fully incorporated. Taste and season with salt as needed. Typically, Japanese mayonnaises are well seasoned and therefore extra salt may not be needed.

To assemble, prepare a small bowl of cold water and add the lemon juice. Then, peel the Nashi pear and slice it in half. Slice thin crescents, discarding any core or seeds, and place the slices into the lemon water to prevent their going brown. Make as many slices as there are slices of tuna. When ready to assemble the dish, drain the pear slices and pat them dry with paper towels.

Then, on a serving plate, arrange the tuna and Nashi pear slices in alternating layers. Place small spoonfuls of grated daikon randomly on top of the tuna and pear. Repeat the process with the wasabi cream, using a squeeze bottle or spoon. Next, carefully dress the dish with Ponzu, being careful not to flood the plate with sauce. Then, garnish with toasted sesame seeds and cress. Serve immediately.

TIPS

» This crudo is best prepared and assembled just before serving.

» Sliced sashimi tuna can be purchased from good fishmongers.

STRAWBERRY PANZANELLA + BURRATA

Mum and I discovered the amazing pairing of strawberries and basil as we watched our favourite chef, Jamie Oliver, one evening. Jamie's programs were actually the introduction to Italian food for both of us and he really influenced the way we experimented with food. We knew nothing more than Bolognese and carbonara, and even then, they were very much bastardised recipes Mum had cut out from magazines or come up with herself. It wasn't until my university days that I discovered authentic Italian home cooking, including the most amazing Tuscan tomato and bread salad called panzanella, thanks to new friends and their very hospitable families. This "panzanella" is not traditional. It brings together the sweet and sour playfulness of strawberries and balsamic vinegar and reminds me of all the faux-Italian deliciousness Mum concocted, borrowing the bravery Jamie inspired. The unexpected addition of sesame oil is the best surprise in aroma and flavour.

Time: 20 minutes | Makes: 4 servings

250 g (9 oz) red strawberries, stems and leaves removed

250 g (9 oz) cherry tomatoes

1 tsp salt, divided

80 g (shy 3 oz) cubed stale bread (cut into large croutons; sourdough is recommended)

3 AUS tbsp or 60 ml or ¼ US cup extra virgin olive oil, plus more to serve

1½ AUS tbsp or 30 ml or 2 US tbsp sherry vinegar

10 ml (2 tsp) toasted sesame oil

½ tsp freshly ground black pepper

½ AUS cup or 42 g or ½ US cup + ½ US tbsp fresh green basil leaves, finely sliced

¼ AUS cup or 16 g or ¼ US cup + ½ tsp fresh dill leaves

¼ AUS cup or 10 g or ¼ US cup + ½ tsp fresh mint leaves, finely sliced

150 g (5.5 oz) burrata

Preheat the oven to 120°C (250°F).

Slice the strawberries and tomatoes at odd angles to obtain a variety of sizes and shapes. Then, place the strawberries, tomatoes and ½ teaspoon of the salt in a bowl and toss to mix thoroughly. Set aside for 10 minutes.

In the meantime, mix together the remaining salt with the croutons and 1 AUS tablespoon (20 ml or 4 teaspoons) of the olive oil in a medium-sized mixing bowl. Place the croutons on a baking tray and bake for 8 to 10 minutes, or until golden and toasted. Remove from the oven and allow to cool.

Drain the liquid from the strawberries and tomatoes into a separate mixing bowl. Add the sherry vinegar, remaining 2 AUS tablespoons (40 ml or 2 US tablespoons + 2 teaspoons) of olive oil, sesame oil and pepper to the strawberry and tomato juice mixture. Stir thoroughly to combine. This is the dressing.

Add one-third of the croutons, half of the herbs and all of the dressing to the strawberries and tomatoes. Toss well. Arrange the dressed strawberries, tomatoes and croutons in the centre of a dish. Place the burrata in the centre on top of the salad. Spread the remaining croutons and herbs around the burrata. Lightly drizzle extra olive oil over the salad and burrata.

TIPS

» Serve this salad with fresh, warm bread or alongside steak or pasta.

» Strawberries can be replaced with peaches, cucumbers, honeydew melon or rockmelon (cantaloupe).

» Balsamic vinegar can also be used for a slightly sweeter variation of the dressing. However, your salad will appear a lot darker and more muddled.

SARDINES ON TOAST

Mum always had a tin of sardines in tomato sauce in the cupboard. She adored tinned fish and this was one of her absolute favourites. She ate it with rice, congee, on toast, on plain crackers or even on its own straight out of the tin. In sixth grade, I had an Italian teacher who talked mostly about his travels everywhere else but Italy. The story that stuck with me was his recount of the white walls of Santorini "emerging like a white pearl from the ocean." He talked about the food; the fragrant lemons and the dried oregano, and how the sardines were eaten head and all! As a 12-year-old with an already big love of food and dreaming of one day travelling the world, I was completely enamoured. This dish is made of the sweetest parts of both these memories.

Time: 15 to 20 minutes | Makes: 4 servings

4 large sardines, butterflied and deboned

3 AUS tbsp or 23 g or 3 US tbsp + ½ tsp plain (all-purpose) flour, seasoned generously with salt

6 AUS tbsp or 120 ml or ½ US cup neutral oil, divided

16 to 20 cherry tomatoes

1 red shallot or ¼ red onion, finely chopped

2 g (2 tsp) dried oregano

⅓ AUS cup or 21 g or ⅓ US cup + ½ tsp finely chopped fresh parsley

1 AUS tbsp or 5 g or 4 tsp finely chopped fresh dill

1 tsp freshly ground black pepper

Juice of 1 lemon

1 AUS tbsp or 20 ml or 4 tsp Maggi Original Seasoning (or 1 tsp light soy sauce plus 1 tsp fish sauce)

4 slices sourdough (or your preferred bread, similar size to the butterflied sardine fillets)

Salted butter

24 to 30 curry leaves, fried in oil until crisp then drained

Coat both sides of the sardine fillets lightly with the seasoned flour. Heat two-thirds of the oil in a medium-sized frying pan over medium-high heat. Once hot, fry the sardine fillets for 60 seconds on each side, then transfer them to a rack over a tray or plate to rest and drain.

Lower the heat beneath the frying pan to medium. Then, add the cherry tomatoes. Shake the pan and let the tomatoes blister and soften for 2 to 3 minutes. Once softened, remove from the heat and transfer them to a medium bowl.

In a separate small bowl, mix together the remaining oil, shallot, oregano, parsley, dill, pepper, lemon juice and Maggi Original Seasoning. Mix thoroughly to combine. Set aside.

Toast the bread, and butter it generously. Then, top each slice of toast with 4 to 5 cherry tomatoes, followed by a sardine fillet, then a generous spoonful of the herb dressing and garnish with crispy curry leaves. Serve while still warm.

TIPS

» Sardines can be replaced with your preferred fish (salmon, tuna, swordfish, whiting, etc.).

» Leftover fresh herbs can be chopped and stored in oil in the fridge to last longer, or frozen in oil to use whenever you need.

» Maggi Seasoning can be replaced with your favourite salty condiment.

» Lao Gan Ma Crispy Chilli Oil drizzled over the top is always welcome.

SCALLOPS WITH LEMON BUTTER AND PONZU

Mum was the biggest lover of butter. Her days as a young nurse when she first moved to Sydney meant a lot of packed cheap meals and snacks like bread and butter with a little bit of salt or jam. It became a habit she never lost. When she was running her own business, she would make herself a "butter sandwich" with slices of butter as thick as you would cut cheese, a few layers of seasoned seaweed all stuck between two slices of white bread. She'd smile like a kid in a candy shop. I've taken Mum's love of butter and seafood and developed this simple recipe. It lets the sweetness of the scallops harmonise with the rich butter, salty soy and aroma of lemon and yuzu. It might be a little unseemly, but I actually let the grill scorch and burn bits of the garlic—I like the bitterness it gives, and it reminds me of flecks of seaweed, just like Mum's naughty sandwiches.

Time: 30 to 35 minutes | Makes: 4 servings (12 scallops)

LEMON BUTTER

200 g or 7 oz or 14 US tbsp salted butter, softened

1 AUS tbsp or 8 g or 4 tsp freshly ground black pepper

Zest and juice of 2 lemons

6 cloves garlic, grated or minced finely

12 large, fresh scallops in half shells

1 AUS cup or 250 ml or 1 US cup + 2 tsp Ponzu (page 24)

In a medium-sized mixing bowl, mix together the lemon butter ingredients until well combined. Then, place in the fridge for 10 to 15 minutes to firm slightly.

Heat a barbecue or grill/broiler to high heat (200°C [400°F]).

Place the scallops on a baking tray lined with aluminium foil if using the grill/broiler function in the oven. Place a heaped teaspoon of the lemon butter on each scallop, then barbecue, shell side down, or grill/broil on the middle rack for 5 to 6 minutes, or until the butter has melted and each scallop is just cooked through.

Serve the scallops immediately, drizzling each with a shy AUS tablespoon (about 18 ml or 3½ teaspoons) of Ponzu.

TIPS

» This recipe works for mussels and large clams in half shells.

» The lemon butter can be stored in an airtight container in the fridge for 3 to 4 weeks, or frozen for 6 months.

» You could also cook the scallops with a food-safe blow torch instead of a barbecue or grill/broiler.

MISO CUCUMBERS AND HERBY COTTAGE CHEESE

Mum's signature sauce (other than her "Everything Sauce" which you can find in my first cookbook, *Sweet, Savory, Spicy*) is a mixture of miso and cumquats (kumquats) she grew in our front yard. The pairing of miso and citrus is terrific. The citrus mellows the saltiness of the miso, and because miso is fermented, it boosts the acidity and "funkiness," creating a mouth-watering flavour. By introducing the hum of garlic and the sweetness and the earthiness of sesame oil to the mixture of miso and yuzu, the marinade becomes full bodied and powerful. Yuzu juice or lemon juice is much easier to source than cumquats, but they both make appropriate substitutions. The cottage cheese really is a celebration of herbs that Mum loved. Dill and mint match the freshness and lightness of the cucumber. Cottage cheese adds texture. This is an all-rounder light dish that goes with everything.

Time: 30 minutes | Makes: 4 servings

3 Lebanese cucumbers, peeled, halved lengthways (lengthwise)

MISO MARINADE

1 AUS tbsp or 21 g or 4 tsp red miso

3 cloves garlic, grated

2 AUS tbsp or 40 ml or 2 US tbsp + 2 tsp rice vinegar

1 AUS tbsp or 20 ml or 4 tsp yuzu juice

1 tsp sugar

1 AUS tbsp or 20 ml or 4 tsp toasted sesame oil

COTTAGE CHEESE

4 AUS tbsp or 75 g or 5 US tbsp + 1 tsp cottage cheese

1 tsp salt, or more as needed

1 tsp freshly ground black pepper

2 AUS tbsp or 4 g or 2 US tbsp + 2 tsp finely chopped fresh mint leaves

2 AUS tbsp or 11 g or 2 US tbsp + 2 tsp finely chopped fresh dill

2 AUS tbsp or 21 g or 2 US tbsp + 2 tsp toasted white sesame seeds

SERVING

Olive oil

Crisp flatbreads or crusty bread

Using a spoon or butter knife, scrape the seeds from the middle of the cucumbers into a medium-sized mixing bowl. Set aside.

Slice the cucumbers into bite-sized pieces. Place the pieces in a large resealable plastic bag.

Combine the miso marinade ingredients in a separate medium-sized mixing bowl, stirring thoroughly until the miso is completely incorporated. Then, add the miso marinade to the cucumbers. Close the bag, ensuring it is securely sealed. Then, massage the marinade into the cucumbers. Once well mixed, store the bag in the fridge for 15 to 20 minutes.

In the meantime, add all the cottage cheese ingredients to the bowl of cucumber seeds. Mix thoroughly. Adjust the salt as needed. Then, spread a generous amount of the cheese mixture on a large platter.

Drain the excess liquid from the bag of cucumbers. Scatter the cucumber pieces over the cottage cheese. Drizzle olive oil over the dish and serve with crisp flatbreads or crusty bread.

SEARED BEEF + GLASS NOODLE SALAD

This is one dish that I was able to share with Mum many years ago and it has been developed and made many times since. This is a crowd-pleaser; my best friend Emilie still requests this dish to be made on occasion. This salad feels light, vibrant and yet fills you up generously. This dish made its debut at a little dinner I cooked for friends back in 2011 and has gone through many different iterations of sauce, protein cuts and types and salad mixes. At one stage it became elaborate and "fancy," but ultimately it has been pared back to its core. As Mum said . . . "the simpler the better." The greatest lesson learnt is that the sauce is the team carrier here. It must be punchy with black vinegar, salty with soy and nutty and silky with sesame oil. The best way to achieve this is with equal parts of each ingredient.

Time: 30 minutes | Makes: 4 servings

BEEF AND GLASS NOODLES

400 g (14 oz) dried mung bean thread noodles (also called glass noodles or "cellophane" noodles)

4 AUS cups or 1 L or 4¼ US cups boiling water

6 cloves garlic, finely minced

⅓ AUS cup or 83 ml or ⅓ US cup + ½ tsp neutral oil, plus more for searing steak

200 g (7 oz) beef rump steak or scotch fillet steak/ribeye (or use your favourite cut of steak)

Salt and freshly ground black pepper

DRESSING

2 AUS tbsp or 40 ml or 2 US tbsp + 2 tsp light soy sauce

2 AUS tbsp or 40 ml or 2 US tbsp + 2 tsp Chinkiang black vinegar

2 AUS tbsp or 40 ml or 2 US tbsp + 2 tsp sesame oil

SALAD

120 g (4 oz) leafy salad mix (use your favourite blend of lettuces, spinach, rocket, etc.)

1 AUS tbsp or 11 g or 4 tsp toasted white sesame seeds

½ AUS cup or 73 g or ½ US cup + 1 tsp toasted cashew nuts

⅓ AUS cup or 25 g or shy 1 oz fried shallots

Soak the noodles in the boiling water in a large bowl for 15 to 20 minutes, stirring occasionally. Once completely transparent and cooked through, drain very well and set aside.

In the meantime, place the minced garlic and neutral oil in a small saucepan over medium-low heat. Allow to fry slowly for 10 to 15 minutes, or until the garlic is lightly golden brown. Then, remove from the heat and set aside to cool.

While the garlic cooks, season your steak liberally with salt and pepper. Heat additional oil in a medium frying pan on high heat. Once the oil is hot, sear the steak for 3 to 4 minutes per side. Once seared, set the steak aside to rest for 5 minutes, then cut into 5-mm (scant ¼-inch)-wide strips. Reserve the resting juices.

In a small mixing bowl or pitcher, mix together the dressing ingredients. Stir thoroughly.

Assemble the salad: To a large mixing bowl, add the drained noodles, sliced steak and resting juices and the salad leaves; toss well to combine. Just before serving, add the dressing and garlic oil as well as the fried garlic, sesame seeds, cashew nuts and fried shallots and toss again to mix well.

TIPS

»   This salad is best served at room temperature.

»   You can pre-make the salad without the dressing a few hours before serving and store it in the fridge. Take the salad out of the fridge 15 minutes before serving. Only add the dressing, sesame seeds, cashew nuts and fried shallots when you are ready to serve.

»   Any cut of steak or other protein can be used. For a completely vegetarian version, use seasoned tofu or even halloumi.

»   Rice vermicelli can be used instead of mung bean thread noodles.

PERSIMMON, RICOTTA + HAZELNUT SALAD
with Nuoc Mam

This is probably the easiest, yet one of the most powerful, salads you will make. In Southeast Asia, it is very common to mix fruits into dishes that use a generous amount of fish sauce or garlic and chilli. The Vietnamese sauce that appears on every table is *nuoc mam*. It is a fish sauce–based dipping sauce with lime, chilli, garlic and sugar. It is a very easy sauce to make and can be used to dip anything and everything into, including sweet or sour fruits.

Time: 10 minutes | Makes: 4 servings

PERSIMMON, RICOTTA + HAZELNUT SALAD

2 persimmons, cut into eighths

1 AUS cup or 260 g or 1 US cup + 2 tsp fresh ricotta, torn into chunks

¼ AUS cup or 35 g or ¼ US cup + ½ tsp hazelnuts, toasted and chopped

NUOC MAM

1 AUS tbsp or 17 g or 4 tsp sugar

3 AUS tbsp or 60 ml or 4 US tbsp warm water

1 AUS tbsp or 20 ml or 4 tsp fresh lime juice

1 AUS tbsp or 20 ml or 4 tsp fish sauce

1 small bird's-eye chilli, thinly sliced

1 clove garlic, thinly sliced

SERVING

Handful of fresh basil leaves

Arrange the cut persimmons, ricotta and hazelnuts randomly on a large platter; set aside in the fridge.

Make the nuoc mam by dissolving the sugar in the warm water in a small mixing bowl. Then, add the lime juice, fish sauce, chilli and garlic. Stir thoroughly to mix well.

When ready to serve, dress the persimmon, ricotta and hazelnuts with the nuoc mam. Garnish with torn basil leaves.

TIP

» Try substituting persimmon with firm peaches, pineapples or melons.

GRILLED BOK CHOY DRESSED IN HARISSA + TAHINI

This dish is simple and stunning. Blending the commonplace Asian leafy green with a few exciting touches of the Middle East, bok choy just becomes a subtly sweet, snappy carrier for the beautiful blend of paprika, garlic, sun-dried tomato and thick tahini. There's no real story behind this dish. It was born out of a craving for something crunchy, light, tasty and saucy. It just happened to be so good that I had to include it in this book.

Time: 45 minutes (if making harissa from scratch) | Makes: 4 servings

HARISSA (SEE TIPS)

10 dried New Mexico chillies (or other large dried chillies with mild to medium spiciness)

7 dried chiles de arbol (increase for more heat, decrease for less heat)

½ AUS cup or 29 g or ½ US cup + 1 tsp sun-dried tomatoes, finely chopped

1 AUS tbsp or 9 g or 4 tsp ground cumin

3.5 g (2 tsp) ground coriander seeds

1 tsp caraway seeds

6 cloves garlic, minced

5 g (2 tsp) ground smoked paprika

1 tsp sea salt

2 AUS tbsp or 40 ml or 2 US tbsp + 2 tsp fresh lemon juice

2 AUS tbsp or 40 ml or 2 US tbsp + 2 tsp white vinegar

¼ AUS cup or 63 ml or ¼ US cup + ½ tsp olive oil

Begin with the harissa. Add the dried New Mexico chillies and chiles de arbol to a mixing bowl and cover with hot water. Place a cover on the bowl and allow the chillies to rehydrate for 20 to 30 minutes.

In the meantime, place the sun-dried tomatoes, cumin, coriander, caraway seeds, garlic, smoked paprika, salt, lemon juice and white vinegar in a food processor. Do not blend yet.

Once the chillies are rehydrated, drain and remove the stems and seeds, then add to the food processor. Blend for 1 to 2 minutes, scraping down the sides as needed, until a smooth paste is achieved. Then, with the food processor running, stream in the olive oil. Taste and adjust the seasoning.

(continued)

TIPS

» You could use store-bought harissa to save time.

» If you make the harissa from scratch, store it in an airtight jar in the fridge for up to 4 weeks. Alternatively, freeze the harissa for up to 6 months.

» The bok choy can be replaced with cabbage wedges, baby cos (romaine) lettuce hearts, even large meaty mushrooms.

» Toasted cashews and pumpkin seeds make a great addition to or substitution for the almonds.

TAHINI SAUCE

¼ AUS cup or 62 g or ¼ US cup +
½ US tbsp tahini

¼ AUS cup or 63 ml or ¼ US cup +
½ tsp water

Juice of 1 lemon

¼ AUS cup or 63 ml or ¼ US cup +
½ tsp pure maple syrup or honey

½ tsp salt

1 tsp freshly ground black pepper

BOK CHOY

2 AUS tbsp or 40 ml or 2 US tbsp +
2 tsp neutral oil

8 heads bok choy, cleaned and halved
lengthwise

Salt

SERVING

⅓ AUS cup or 38 g or ⅓ US cup +
½ tsp toasted slivered almonds

Fresh lemon juice and zest

⅓ AUS cup or 6 g or ⅓ US cup +
¼ tsp fresh coriander (cilantro) leaves

Mix together all the ingredients for the tahini sauce in a small bowl.

Cook the bok choy: Drizzle 1 to 2 AUS tablespoons (20 to 40 ml or 4 to 8 teaspoons) of oil over the bok choy, massaging in the oil with your hands. In a dry griddle (grill) pan over high heat, place the oiled bok choy cut side down and allow it to char for 3 to 4 minutes. Flip the bok choy and cook for another 3 to 4 minutes, or until softened and well charred. Transfer the bok choy to a tray and season generously with salt.

Plate the bok choy on a large platter. Dress liberally with the tahini sauce and then big dollops of harissa. Drizzle on some of the oil from the harissa as a finishing touch and garnish with toasted almonds, lemon juice, lemon zest and fresh coriander leaves.

SWEET AND SOUR PORK + PRAWN SALAD

While I was growing up, Mum's salads were always packed with textures and unique flavours. Tamarind was a huge hit with any salad she made using meat or shellfish. This is my version of *moo nam tok*, a classic Thai salad of grilled pork, vibrant and pungent herbs, lots of lime and Mum's generous touch of tamarind. Discovering salads throughout Southeast Asia was eye-opening. There's no set definition of what should be in a salad, but the common denominator is texture. The addition of the ground toasted glutinous rice (called *khao khua* in Thai) provides nuttiness and texture. The pork and prawns perfectly complement the soft herbs. The sides of fresh vegetables provide another layer of texture. It's quite a complex orchestra of flavours, yet the dish itself is so simply prepared.

Time: 45 minutes | Makes: 4 servings

PORK AND PRAWN SALAD

300 g (10.5 oz) pork scotch fillets (also called scotch steaks or pork neck steaks)

1 AUS tbsp or 20 ml or 4 tsp neutral oil

150 g (5.5 oz) cooked and peeled prawns (shrimp)

¼ AUS cup or 42 g or ¼ US cup + ½ tsp finely sliced Asian red shallots

½ AUS cup or 21 g or ½ US cup + 1 tsp fresh mint leaves

3 AUS tbsp or 4 g or 4 US tbsp finely sliced fresh sawtooth coriander or regular coriander (cilantro)

¼ AUS cup or 14 g or ¼ US cup + 1 tsp sliced spring onion (scallions)

PORK MARINADE

1 AUS tbsp or 20 ml or 4 tsp fish sauce

1 tsp dark brown sugar

½ tsp freshly ground black pepper

1 tsp ground ginger

For the pork and prawn salad, place the pork on a large, clean, sturdy surface. Use a meat mallet or rolling pin to lightly pound the pork steaks to about 6 mm (¼ inch) thick, then transfer them to a large resealable plastic bag or large mixing bowl.

Mix together the pork marinade ingredients in a small mixing bowl and then pour the marinade over the pork. Massage the marinade into the pork and leave to marinate for at least 30 minutes or overnight.

Heat the oil in a large frying pan over medium-high heat and cook the pork for 3 to 4 minutes on each side, or until just cooked. Remove from the heat and allow to rest before cutting into thin slices. Reserve any resting juices.

(continued)

TIPS

»   Using glutinous or sticky rice will give you a softer rice powder that creates a thick and soft coating for the finished salad. If glutinous rice is unavailable, you can still use regular long-grain or jasmine rice to add a similar toasty flavour with a slightly crunchier texture.

»   Sawtooth coriander is a type of Thai fresh herb. If unavailable, you can use regular coriander or simply leave it out.

»   Snake beans can be found at Asian markets. Alternatively, replace snake beans with regular green beans.

SALAD DRESSING

1 AUS tbsp or 10 g or 4 tsp uncooked glutinous rice (also called sweet Thai rice)

2 AUS tbsp or 40 ml or 2 US tbsp + 2 tsp Sweet + Sour Tamarind Sauce (page 20)

1 AUS tbsp or 20 ml or 4 tsp fish sauce

9 g (2 tsp) sugar

1 AUS tbsp or 20 ml or 4 tsp fresh lime juice

SERVING

¼ small cabbage, cut into a wedge

½ AUS cup or 48 g or 1.5 oz sliced snake beans (cut into 5-cm [2"] lengths)

Sliced cucumber

While the pork rests, start the dressing: Toast the glutinous rice in a small, dry frying pan over medium-high heat until golden brown (approximately 5 to 6 minutes), shaking or stirring frequently. Remove the rice from the heat and allow to cool. Then, use a mortar and pestle or spice grinder to finely grind the rice. Combine the Sweet + Sour Tamarind Sauce, fish sauce, sugar and lime juice in a bowl and stir to dissolve the sugar. Add the toasted rice powder and stir again.

In a large bowl, combine the warm pork slices and prawns with the sliced shallots. Add the dressing and toss until well combined. Then add the mint, coriander and spring onion and lightly toss. Transfer to a serving plate with cabbage, snake beans and sliced cucumber.

SPICY CHICKEN + JELLYFISH SALAD

I debated whether to include this recipe in the book because I haven't innovated or twisted this classic Chinese recipe at all. It's a very straightforward recipe. I decided to include it because it is probably my favourite salad in the world. It is a deeply emotional recipe to me that makes me long for home and childhood. My mother would go out of her way to source big, crunchy, glistening pieces of jellyfish for me when I was a child. It has the most satisfying texture, and the recipe demonstrates such simple yet effective use of the sauces in the staple pantry. For those that are unfamiliar with jellyfish, I eagerly encourage you to head to an Asian grocery store and pick up a few packets. Give this recipe a go! This salad is so full of character and uniqueness.

Time: 20 minutes | Makes: 4 servings

CHICKEN AND JELLYFISH SALAD

280 g (10 oz) instant (packaged) unflavoured jellyfish, soaked in cold water for 1 hour

300 g (10.5 oz) chicken breast

1 Lebanese cucumber, shredded

½ AUS cup or 8 g or ½ US cup + ½ tsp fresh coriander (cilantro) leaves

70 to 75 g (2.5 to 3 oz) sugar snap peas, trimmed and sliced

¼ AUS cup or 39 g or ¼ US cup + 1 tsp toasted unsalted peanuts

1 AUS tbsp or 11 g or 1 US tbsp + 1 tsp toasted white sesame seeds

DRESSING

2 AUS tbsp or 40 ml or 2 US tbsp + 2 tsp Lao Gan Ma Crispy Chilli Oil

2 AUS tbsp or 40 ml or 2 US tbsp + 2 tsp Chinkiang black vinegar

1 AUS tbsp or 20 ml or 4 tsp light soy sauce

10 ml (2 tsp) sesame oil

SERVING

Finely sliced spring onion (scallion)

Store-bought fried shallots

While the jellyfish is soaking, place the chicken breast in a medium-sized saucepan and add cold water until it just covers the chicken breast. Place the saucepan over medium heat and bring to a simmer for 2 minutes. Place a lid on the saucepan, turn off the heat and leave the chicken to poach for 14 minutes.

Once the chicken has cooked through, remove it from the saucepan and leave it to cool. Once cool to the touch, shred the chicken using forks or slice thinly. Then, place the chicken, cucumber, coriander, sugar snap peas, peanuts and sesame seeds in a large mixing bowl.

Once the jellyfish has soaked, rinse it very well, then pat it dry. Slice the jellyfish into small strips and add them to the bowl with the chicken.

Mix together all the dressing ingredients in a separate small bowl. Then, pour the dressing over the chicken and jellyfish salad. Toss the salad really well to mix thoroughly.

Serve the salad in a dish, pouring any excess dressing over it and garnishing with spring onion and fried shallots.

TIPS

» Jellyfish can be purchased in packets from most Asian grocery stores.

» For a vegetarian version, replace the chicken and jellyfish with pressed firm tofu and konjac (elephant yam).

» The jellyfish can be replaced with an additional chicken breast for a version of this salad without seafood.

» The Lao Gan Ma Crispy Chilli oil can be replaced with a bit of garlic oil and more sesame oil, for a non-spicy version.

» Jellyfish can be stored in an airtight container in the fridge for up to a week.

» The salad, undressed, can be made a day ahead.

» Try adding other salad leaves or vegetables.

PANI SPRING ROLLS

I'll admit it. This recipe is a bastardisation, an adaptation. It's a hack recipe designed to be some easier version of legitimate *pani puri*. It is genius. It also reminds me of my mother's approach to re-creating recipes with a few creative liberties through and through. The first time I ate pani puri was in a fine dining modern Indian-inspired restaurant in an alleyway in Melbourne. The crisp hollow semolina shell (puri) was light and had a bubbled and blistered exterior. The top was cracked open and the hollow was filled with an incredible assortment of ingredients: potato, chickpeas, onion, mint, coriander, spices. It was served with a jug of chilled sweet and sour rose water (*panito*). My version borrows some of the elements of the Bengali pani puri, also known as *fuchka*, which was introduced to me by my good friend Rashedul during an Eid celebration. Specifically, the combination of eggs and tamarind. The spring roll pastry imitates the light crispness of puri, and the thin sweet and sour pomegranate sauce is perfect for dipping the rolls into. This is the snack I wish I could have made for Mum.

Time: 45 minutes | Makes: 4 servings (16 medium-sized spring rolls)

SPRING ROLLS AND FILLING

2 large potatoes, peeled and diced into 5-mm (scant ¼") cubes

2 AUS tbsp or 40 ml or 2 US tbsp + 2 tsp ghee or neutral oil

1 medium-sized brown onion, finely diced

240 g (8.5 oz) drained tinned chickpeas

1 tsp ground coriander seeds

1 tsp ground cumin

1 tsp ground red chilli

9 g (1½ tsp) salt

4 large hard-boiled eggs, finely chopped

2 green serrano chillies, finely chopped

2 AUS tbsp or 3 g or 2½ US tbsp finely chopped fresh coriander (cilantro)

2 AUS tbsp or 7 g or 2½ US tbsp finely chopped fresh mint

Neutral oil, for frying

16 sheets spring roll pastry (wrappers); 21.5 cm x 21.5 cm (8½" x 8½")

POMEGRANATE PANI

¾ AUS cup or 187 ml or ¾ US cup + 2 tsp pomegranate juice

1 AUS tbsp or 20 ml or 4 tsp rose water

9 g (2 tsp) caster (superfine) sugar

½ tsp salt

For the spring rolls, boil the diced potato in a pot of boiling salted water over medium-high heat for 5 to 6 minutes, or until tender. Drain well and let air dry.

Heat the ghee in a large frying pan or wok over medium-high heat. Once the ghee is hot, stir-fry the onion for 20 to 30 seconds just until it begins to colour. Then, add the potatoes, chickpeas, ground coriander seed, ground cumin, ground red chilli and salt. Stir-fry for 2 to 3 minutes, then remove from the heat. Transfer the mixture to a medium-sized mixing bowl.

Take one-third of the potato and chickpea mixture and place it in a separate mixing bowl. Use a potato masher or heavy object to coarsely crush the mixture. You don't want a paste, but it should be roughly mashed. Transfer this mashed mixture back to the remaining two-thirds of the potato and chickpea mixture. Once cool, add the eggs, chillies, coriander and mint. Stir thoroughly to combine.

Fill a medium-sized saucepan with neutral oil to a depth of 4 cm (1½ inches) and place it over medium heat (see Tip). Take a sheet of spring roll pastry and place it in a diamond shape in front of you. Place 2 AUS tablespoons (40 ml or 2 US tablespoons + 2 teaspoons) of the filling in a line on the lower third closest to you. Roll the corner of the pastry closest to you over the filling, fold in the two corners on the sides and roll tightly up to the remaining corner farthest away from you so you have a spring roll shape. Repeat with the remaining filling and pastry.

Fry 3 to 4 spring rolls at a time for 2 to 3 minutes, rotating frequently so they evenly brown. Remove the spring rolls to a rack set over a tray to drain.

In a small bowl, mix together the ingredients for the pomegranate pani, whisking until the salt and sugar dissolve. Serve the spring rolls hot with the dipping sauce.

TIP

»   The frying oil should not be too hot, otherwise the pastry will burn quickly. An easy way to test if the oil is hot enough for frying is to place a dry handle of a wooden spoon or wooden chopstick into the oil. If it very actively bubbles around the wood, the oil is hot enough. Alternatively, use a temperature-safe thermometer to check that the temperature of the oil is 160°C (320°F).

SOMETHING SWEET

My kind of desserts are sweet with a little hint of savoury. The salty, nutty, acidic components are necessary to balance out the sweetness. The other key feature you'll find in this chapter is that all the desserts have a variety of textures, like crunchy or crispy, to interrupt anything creamy. For me, that's where the excitement is; a variety of temperatures, textures, colours and flavours. A lot of these desserts are inspired by French and Italian dessert elements, and this chapter is probably where my love of those cuisines shines strongly. Fusing in Asian flavours is a joy and brings something unexpected to the recipe. I think the concept of fusion food is divisive. There are those that think it compromises one or more of the culinary identities, and others that think it's an expression of creativity. I fall into the latter camp. Blending, mixing and fusing cuisines is closer to the reality of how people eat and live than keeping things strictly to tradition. I think a lot of people would be surprised to find out exactly how their most loved traditional dishes developed through history. But, enough with that debate. This chapter represents fun, surprise and joy.

HONEY + MILK PANNA COTTA

Whenever I was sick, had trouble sleeping or simply needed some comfort in the middle of the night, Mum would heat up a small mug of milk in the microwave and stir in some honey. She'd cuddle me as I sipped the sweet milk and eventually fell asleep in her arms. It is one of the most precious memories I have, and both the smell and taste of honey and milk together always brings me back to that time. This recipe brings together that warm, comforting experience with the light, creamy, silky elegance of panna cotta and little bursts of sweetness from the honey pearls. This dessert looks impressive and warms the heart at the same time.

Time: 40 minutes cooking plus 4 hours setting time | Makes: 4 servings

PANNA COTTA

4½ gold-strength gelatine leaves

500 ml (2 US cups + 2 US tbsp) thickened (heavy) cream

200 ml (¾ US cup + 4 tsp) milk

90 g (¼ US cup + 3 US tbsp) caster (superfine) sugar

150 g (½ US cup + 2 US tbsp) honey

HONEY PEARLS (SEE TIP)

3 AUS tbsp or 60 ml or ¼ US cup honey

½ AUS cup or 125 ml or ½ US cup + 1 tsp water

2 g (⅔ tsp) agar agar

2 AUS cups or 500 ml or 2 US cups + 2 US tbsp neutral oil, refrigerated in a tall measuring cup for at least 2 hours

MILK CRUMB

75 g (5 US tbsp + 1 tsp) salted butter

125 g (¾ US cup + 2½ US tbsp) skim (non-fat) milk powder

1¼ AUS tbsp or 22 g or 1½ US tbsp + ½ tsp caster (superfine) sugar

¼ tsp salt

SERVING

Edible flowers (marigolds, violas, snapdragons)

For the panna cotta, soak the gelatine in a bowl of cold water until softened, about 5 minutes. Combine the cream, milk, sugar and honey in a saucepan over medium heat and bring to a simmer, stirring to dissolve the sugar, then remove from the heat. Squeeze any excess water from the gelatine, then stir the gelatine into the cream mixture until dissolved. Strain the mixture into a pitcher, then pour it into four dessert bowls and refrigerate until set (minimum 4 hours). The panna cotta can be made up to 2 days ahead.

For the honey pearls, place the honey and water in a small saucepan over medium heat. Warm gently and stir until the honey dissolves. Then, dissolve the agar agar into the honey mixture. Stir well and bring to a boil. Remove from the heat and allow to cool for 4 to 5 minutes, but not enough to start gelling together.

Prepare a bowl of water and ice. Take the cold oil from the fridge. Using a syringe or dropper (see Tip), draw the honey up and then make droplets into the cold oil. Let the pearls fall to the bottom of the vessel and firm up for a few seconds. Then, use a small slotted spoon to fish the pearls out and place them in the bowl of water and ice. When ready to serve, use the small slotted spoon to remove the pearls from the water and put them on a paper towel to drain off any excess moisture.

For the milk crumb, preheat the oven to 150°C (300°F).

Melt the butter in a medium-sized microwave-safe container until warm and fully liquid. Then, stir in the skim milk powder. Stir in the caster sugar and salt until well combined.

Spread the crumb mixture on a lined baking tray and bake for 8 to 10 minutes, or until golden brown.

Serve each panna cotta with a scoop of crumb on top, plus some pearls and edible flowers.

TIP

» For the honey pearls, you will need a clean syringe without a needle point. These are available at cookware stores or through a pharmacy.

MANGO PANCAKES

Yum cha (also known as dim sum), a Cantonese dining experience where carts topped with bite-sized dishes, dumplings, noodles, vegetables and an assortment of sweets are served to waiting diners, has been a consistent, joyful, comforting part of my culture and journey as a chef. It is where bellies have been satisfied on Sunday brunches, big announcements have been made over a steamer basket of *har gow*, arguments have been had over chicken feet and beef tendons, hangovers have been cured by pork buns and inspiration has been taken from the multitude of mouth-watering artistic creations on rickety trolleys. One of the best parts of yum cha is the cold, refreshing dessert you order, even though you're so full you're bursting at the seams, because the relief the cold sweetness brings is absolute heaven. Controversially, I believe mango pancakes are superior to mango puddings. Both are signature yum cha desserts, but the mango pancake is the best. The sweetened vanilla whipped cream encasing a sweet piece of firm mango, all wrapped up in a slightly tacky, elastic pancake is the perfect bundle of joy. It's like a dessert dumpling or spring roll that makes total sense after several rounds of the savoury kinds.

Time: 1 hour + 30 minutes chilling | Makes: 4 servings (12 pancakes)

PANCAKE BATTER

6 large eggs

¼ AUS cup or 52 g or ¼ US cup + ½ tsp caster (superfine) sugar

1 AUS cup or 250 ml or 1 US cup + 2 tsp milk

¼ AUS cup or 63 ml or ¼ US cup + ½ tsp neutral oil, plus more for frying

1 tsp vanilla extract (optional)

1 AUS cup or 130 g or 1 US cup + 2 tsp plain (all-purpose) flour

½ tsp salt

10 drops yellow food colouring (optional)

FILLING

300 ml (1¼ US cups + 1 tsp) thickened (heavy) cream

¼ AUS cup or 125 g or 1 US cup + 2 tsp pure icing (confectioners') sugar

2 ripe mangoes, pitted and sliced

For the batter, whisk together the eggs and sugar in a small bowl and then add the milk, oil and vanilla. Sift together the flour and salt in a separate bowl. Then, gradually pour in the egg mixture, whisking continuously. Add the yellow food colouring, and whisk again until incorporated evenly. Sieve the mixture into another bowl to remove any remaining lumps, cover and allow to stand for 10 to 20 minutes at room temperature. The mixture will appear thinner than a regular pancake batter.

Heat a large non-stick frying pan over low heat and brush the pan with a very thin layer of oil. Pour in a few AUS tablespoons (20 ml or 4 teaspoons per tablespoon) of the batter and then tilt and swirl the pan so the batter coats the entire base of the pan in a thin layer. Place a cover over the pan and allow the pancake to cook for 2 to 3 minutes, or until the top is dry to the touch. Do not brown the pancake too much and do not flip the pancake. Transfer the pancake to a plate and repeat for the remaining batter. Let the pancakes cool completely.

For the filling, whip the cream and icing sugar together in a large bowl until stiff peaks form. Peel the mangos and slice the mango cheeks into thick batons. Place both the whipped cream and the mango in the freezer for around 15 minutes to firm.

Spoon a little whipped cream onto the fried side of each pancake and top with one to two slices of mango. Then, carefully roll up the pancake like a spring roll or a burrito. Chill in the fridge for at least 10 minutes before serving.

BLACK SESAME AND GINGER CRÉMEUX,

with Blackberries and Soy Sauce Peanut Praline

This is my favourite dessert I've ever made. Partially because it allowed me to win Dish of the Day during *MasterChef Australia* 2017 at a Michelin-starred restaurant takeover in Tokyo, but mostly because it was the revelation moment, the enlightenment point where I understood my own style of desserts and what played to my strengths and preferences in the pastry world. This dessert is dark, mysterious, surprising and textural. It blends French technique with iconic Asian flavours. This has developed a little further than when I made it on TV to become the best version yet. It is simple to make and visually stunning.

Time: 30 minutes + 1 hour freezing | Makes: 4 to 6 servings

BLACK SESAME AND GINGER CRÉMEUX

2 large egg yolks

1 large egg

45 g (1.5 oz) caster (superfine) sugar

125 ml (½ US cup + 1 tsp) thickened (heavy) cream

2 AUS tbsp or 40 g or 2 US tbsp + 2 tsp black sesame paste

3.5 g (2 tsp) ground ginger

3.5 g (⅛ oz) gold-strength gelatine sheets, softened in cold water, drained and squeezed

50 g (3½ US tbsp) unsalted butter

PICKLED GINGER

2 AUS tbsp or 35 g or 2 US tbsp + 2 tsp caster (superfine) sugar

½ AUS cup or 125 ml or ½ US cup + 1 tsp white vinegar

Pinch of salt

15 g (0.5 oz) fresh ginger root, peeled and sliced into very fine julienne

SOY SAUCE PEANUT PRALINE

100 g (3.5 oz) peanuts, lightly toasted

1 AUS tbsp or 20 ml or 4 tsp soy sauce

1 AUS tbsp or 17 g or 4 tsp caster (superfine) sugar

15 g (1 US tbsp) unsalted butter, melted

SERVING

6 to 8 blackberries per serving

For the crémeux, place the egg yolks, egg and sugar in a medium-sized mixing bowl and whisk until pale and fluffy.

Separately, in a saucepan over medium heat, whisk together the cream, black sesame paste and ground ginger until fully incorporated and bring to almost a simmer. Remove from the heat.

Add the hot cream mixture a little at a time to the egg mixture, whisking constantly. Once all the hot cream mixture has been whisked in, pour the combined egg mixture back into the saucepan and place over low heat. Stir constantly until thickened and the mixture can coat the back of a spoon. Make sure to scrape the bottom and sides of the saucepan.

Remove the saucepan from the heat, then add the drained and squeezed gelatine and use a stick blender to thoroughly incorporate or whisk extremely well. Add the butter, little by little, mixing with the stick blender or whisking extremely well.

Pour the crémeux base through a sieve into a 19 x 9–cm (7½ x 3½–inch) loaf pan lined with cling film (plastic wrap). Place the crémeux into the freezer for 1 hour or until set. Slice into 4 to 6 servings.

For the pickled ginger, combine the sugar with the vinegar and salt in a small saucepan and bring to a simmer over medium heat. Whisk to dissolve the sugar. Remove the pickling liquid from the heat and add the julienned ginger after 1 to 2 minutes. Allow to cool.

For the praline, in a pan over medium-high heat, combine the toasted peanuts and soy sauce. Toss until all the peanuts are coated and the soy sauce begins to evaporate, about 3 to 4 minutes. Add the caster sugar and melted butter, tossing to coat the peanuts and melt the sugar. Remove from the heat and allow to cool completely. Transfer to a food processor and blitz until crumbly.

Place a serving of the crémeux in the centre of each plate. Top with a generous spoon of the praline over the top and then finish with blackberries and the pickled ginger.

TIPS

» Using electric whisks and stick blenders is highly recommended. This saves time and takes less physical effort.

» Other fruits that work well include red or black plums and cherries.

MATCHA AND COCONUT SEMIFREDDO, TOASTED RICE AND RASPBERRIES

Bittersweet, grassy matcha blended with creamy smooth coconut has to be one of the sexiest flavour combinations ever. This semifreddo is very easy to make and very addictive to eat. I hope you'll find yourself, like me, taking little spoonfuls of it in the middle of the night just as a little treat as you pass the freezer. The toasted rice is absolutely imperative to this full plated dessert, though. It is like a completely elevated level of popcorn. It's crunchy, nutty, so aromatic and brings to the semifreddo the best kind of contrast. Raspberries bring to the dessert a pop of colour, a little sweetness and sometimes tartness. This is a very balanced, clean, light dessert.

Time: 45 minutes + 8 hours freezing | Makes: 4 servings

Oil, for pan

1 AUS cup or 89 g or 1 US cup + 2 tsp desiccated coconut

SEMIFREDDO

125 g (4.5 oz) double (heavy) cream

125 g (4.5 oz) high-quality coconut cream, separated from coconut oil (see Tips)

1 AUS tbsp or 8 g or 4 tsp high-grade matcha powder

4 large eggs (200 g [7 oz])

100 g (½ US cup) sugar

¼ tsp salt

TOASTED RICE

½ AUS cup or 104 g or ½ US cup + 1 tsp uncooked glutinous rice (sweet Thai rice)

SERVING

5 to 6 raspberries per serving

For the semifreddo, lightly grease a 19 x 9–cm (7½ x 3½–inch) loaf pan with oil and line with cling film (plastic wrap). Then, sprinkle the desiccated coconut in a thin layer to completely cover the base of the loaf pan.

In the bowl of a stand mixer fitted with the whisk attachment, or by hand in a large bowl with a whisk, whip the double cream, coconut cream and matcha powder until soft peaks form. Do not over-whip.

Fill a small saucepan with about 2.5 cm (1 inch) of water and place over medium heat.

In the bowl of a stand mixer or a large heat-proof mixing bowl, combine the eggs, sugar and salt. Place the bowl over the pot of water on the stove, making sure the bottom of the bowl doesn't touch the water. Whisk constantly and cook the egg mixture over the double boiler until it reaches 74°C (165°F). This will take approximately 10 to 15 minutes and the mixture will be custardy and thickened.

When the eggs reach temperature, transfer the bowl to the stand mixer fitted with the whisk attachment or manually whisk. Whip on high speed until the mixture becomes even thicker, foamy and triples in volume, about 5 to 8 minutes by machine or 10 to 15 minutes by hand. You should be able to use the whisk to draw a figure-eight in the batter. Add half of the whipped cream into the whipped eggs and gently fold until fully combined. Then, repeat with the remaining whipped cream. Transfer the mixture to the prepared loaf pan and cover well with cling film. Place in the freezer and freeze until firm, about 8 hours, or ideally overnight.

To make the toasted rice, place the rice in a small, dry frying pan over medium heat. Toast over 15 to 20 minutes, or until deeply golden brown. Allow to cool to the touch, then grind in a spice grinder or mortar and pestle until very fine.

Once the semifreddo is frozen, carefully remove from the loaf pan, slice and serve with a sprinkling of toasted rice and fresh raspberries.

TIPS

» Using electric whisks and stick blenders is highly recommended. This saves time and takes less physical effort.

» Coconut cream can be separated from the coconut oil by placing the tin of coconut cream in the freezer for 15 to 20 minutes. Then, simply scoop the cream off the top.

» The semifreddo can be kept frozen in the freezer for 3 to 4 weeks.

APPLE AND CUCUMBER PAVLOVA

with Shiso Granita

Green is the colour associated with freshness, herbaceousness, liveliness and refreshing cold temperatures. These are all characteristics of this dessert. Shiso brings an aniseed-like sweetness, and when paired with mint, the granita is the best thing to munch on during a warm day. The apple and cucumber mixture is really fresh, tart and cooling. You can pair this with whatever style of meringue you like: soft and marshmallowy, crisp outside with a chewy centre or, my favourite, absolutely crisp and light all the way through. The real heart of this dessert is a contrast in sweet and sour.

Time: 30 minutes + 2 hours baking | Makes: 4 to 6 servings

MERINGUE NESTS (SEE TIPS)

3 large egg whites, at room temperature

¾ AUS cup or 156 g or ¾ US cup + 1½ tsp granulated sugar

1 tsp fresh lemon juice (see "Apple and Cucumber Filling" ingredients below)

1 tsp vanilla extract

1 tsp corn starch

SHISO GRANITA

8 large shiso leaves

½ AUS cup loosely packed or 20 g or ½ US cup fresh mint leaves

1 AUS tbsp or 17 g or 4 US tsp caster (superfine) sugar

2 AUS cups or 500 ml or 2 US cups + 2 US tbsp water

APPLE AND CUCUMBER FILLING

2 small green apples, finely diced into 5-mm (scant ¼") cubes

1 Lebanese cucumber, finely diced into 5-mm (scant ¼") cubes

Juice of 1 lemon (you can extract the tsp of lemon juice for the Meringue Nests from here)

SERVING

200 ml (¾ US cup + 2 tsp) crème fraîche

Edible flowers (marigolds, nasturtiums, violas)

Preheat the oven to 100°C (212°F). Begin with the meringue nests: Line a large baking sheet with parchment paper. Using a stand mixer fitted with the whisk attachment, beat the egg whites on high speed until soft peaks form, 1 to 2 minutes. With the mixer on, gradually add the granulated sugar and beat on high speed for 10 minutes, or until stiff peaks that are smooth and glossy form. Use a spatula to quickly fold in the lemon juice, vanilla and corn starch. Mix until fully incorporated.

Pipe the meringue into 8- to 9-cm (3- to 3½-inch)-wide rounds onto the parchment paper and indent the centre of each round with a spoon to create a nest shape. Bake for 90 minutes, then turn off the oven and, without opening the door, let the meringue nests sit in the hot oven for another 30 to 40 minutes. Transfer the meringue nests with their parchment paper onto the counter or a cooling rack to cool to room temperature once fully baked.

In the meantime, to make the shiso granita, blanch the shiso and mint leaves in boiling water for 20 seconds, then immediately transfer to ice water. Drain well, then blitz the leaves with the remaining shiso granita ingredients in a blender until fully combined and the leaves are finely blended. Set in a container or tray and freeze for 3 to 4 hours or until completely frozen.

About 10 minutes before you are ready to serve, mix together all the ingredients for the apple and cucumber filling in a small mixing bowl. Set aside in the fridge for a few minutes to chill.

When ready to serve, place a meringue nest on each serving plate, followed by a dollop of crème fraîche on top of each meringue. Then, drain the apple and cucumber filling very well and add a couple of spoonfuls of the filling on top of the crème fraîche. Using a fork, scrape the surface of the frozen granita to create a snow effect. Then, spoon the shaved granita over the filling. Garnish with flowers and serve immediately.

TIPS

» An electric stand mixer is highly recommended for this recipe; however, it is doable by hand, but keep in mind that it will take significantly longer.

» The meringue nests can be made up to 48 hours in advance. Once completely cooled, keep the nests in an airtight container out of sunlight and out of the fridge. The shiso granita can be made up to 1 week in advance, stored in the freezer.

» Store-bought pre-made meringue nests are completely acceptable and save a lot of time and effort.

LYCHEE + ROSE TARTLETS

One of my favourite ice cream flavours is lychee and rose. I discovered it during high school at a small, Instagram-worthy ice cream shop beneath an arcade. It was probably one of the only sweet-on-sweet desserts I liked. It was perfect with a wafer cone. I had it again as an adult a couple of years ago and I could barely get through half of it because it was so sweet, yet that floral sweetness and aroma was so captivating. This recipe is a little spin on that ice cream and definitely tempers the sweetness. Plus, these tart shells are quite surprising! Spring roll pastry is essentially a water-based pastry much like *brik* or phyllo. This means that it's ideal for crisping up and can be made very, very thin. It's an added element of delicacy to this recipe.

Time: 25 to 30 minutes | Makes: 4 servings (12 tartlets)

TART SHELLS

Store-bought spring roll pastry (wrappers); 21.5 cm x 21.5 mm (8½" x 8½")

2 AUS tbsp or 40 ml or 2 US tbsp + 2 tsp neutral oil

MASCARPONE FILLING

250 g (9 oz) mascarpone

1 AUS tbsp or 11 g or 4 tsp pure icing (confectioners') sugar

¼ tsp salt

1 tsp rosewater

Zest of 1 lemon

SERVING

560 g (20 oz) tinned lychees in syrup, drained and thinly sliced

Dried edible rose petals

Preheat the oven to 180°C (350°F).

For the tart shells, peel off two layers of the spring roll pastry at a time and place them on a flat hard surface. Use an 8.5-cm (3¼-inch) circular cookie cutter or ring mould to cut circles out of the pastry. Repeat until you have 12 circles.

Brush a thin layer of oil on six 6.5-cm (2½-inch) tart moulds or the wells of a muffin tray. Place a disc of pastry on each one, then brush the top of the pastry lightly with oil. Next, place another set of tart moulds or a muffin tray on top of the pastry, sandwiching the pastry between the moulds or trays.

Place the doubled trays of tart shells in the oven to bake for 15 minutes, or until golden brown. Then, transfer to a cooling rack to cool completely.

In the meantime, whisk together all the ingredients for the mascarpone filling.

Pipe or spoon the filling into the tart shells. Then, top with the sliced lychees and dried rose petals. Serve immediately.

TIPS

» If you find the tart shells too thin, simply use three layers of the spring roll pastry.

» If the mascarpone filling becomes too thin, mix in 15 grams (1 US tablespoon) of mascarpone at a time until thickened. If it is too thick, add a teaspoon or two (5 to 10 ml) of fresh lemon juice or even a little of the lychee syrup.

» The lychee syrup can be reserved for use in other recipes, cocktails or even granitas.

CHOCOLATE, WALNUT AND FIVE-SPICE TART

with Crème Fraîche

My best friend Emilie has a love of rich, deep, heavy chocolate desserts. If something rich and chocolatey is on the menu for dessert, she's ordering it. I'm a bit of the opposite; I prefer light, mousse-like, airy chocolate desserts with something salty or citrusy. But every time I create a chocolate recipe, I think of Emilie and how satisfied she would be if she ate it. This tart is basically an ode to Emilie and her love of chocolate. It is luxurious, textural, sticky, dense, bold, and the subtle hints of Chinese five-spice powder add extra warmth. The crème fraîche is the touch of lightness that's needed to help you get past the third bite. The walnuts are purely for my own textural satisfaction and complement the almonds used in the tart shell.

Time: 2 hours | Makes: 8 to 10 servings

PASTRY

260 g (9 oz) plain (all-purpose) flour, plus more for dusting

100 g (3.5 oz) icing (confectioners') sugar

30 g (1 oz) ground almonds

125 g (8 US tbsp + 2½ tsp) unsalted butter

3 large eggs, divided

1 tsp milk

DARK CHOCOLATE FILLING

175 g (¾ US cup) demerara sugar

150 g (5.5 oz) golden syrup

50 g (3½ US tbsp) salted butter

1 tsp Chinese five-spice powder

75 g (2.5 oz) dark chocolate, roughly chopped

1 tsp milk

3 large eggs

150 g (5.5 oz) walnuts, toasted and roughly chopped

SERVING

Crème fraîche or plain Greek yoghurt

Preheat the oven to 180°C (350°F).

To make the pastry, place the flour, sugar, ground almonds and butter in a large bowl. Use your fingertips to mix them together into a crumb consistency. Add two of the eggs and mix well with a spatula, then cover and let rest in the fridge for 30 minutes.

Lightly dust a work surface with flour. Roll out the pastry until about 2 mm (⅟₁₆ inch) thick and use it to line a 25-cm (9¾-inch) springform tart ring, letting any excess hang over the sides. Cover the pastry base with baking parchment and rice or baking beans. Blind bake for 20 minutes, or until the base is cooked through and lightly golden.

Remove the rice or baking beans and the baking parchment. Mix together the remaining egg and milk in a small bowl. Use a pastry brush to egg wash the tart, then return to the oven for a further 3 minutes. Remove the tart shell from the oven and set aside.

Lower the oven temperature to 170°C (325°F).

For the chocolate filling, heat the demerara sugar, golden syrup and butter together in a pan over medium-high heat until it begins to boil, whisk in the Chinese five-spice, then add the dark chocolate, milk and eggs. Stir thoroughly to combine well, then remove the mixture from the heat.

Place the walnuts in the pre-cooked tart case and pour the chocolate through a sieve over the walnuts. Bake for 40 minutes. Remove from the oven and let cool before serving with a dollop of crème fraîche or Greek yoghurt.

JASMINE AND CONDENSED MILK ICE CREAM

with Brown Butter Panko

When I was in primary school and early high school, some school holiday mornings were spent going to work with Mum. We'd leave very early in the morning and I just wouldn't be able to wake up for breakfast. So, I'd have breakfast with Mum and my uncle in the break room. One of the most memorable breakfasts was a bagel, split in half, toasted until perfectly peanut brown, then spread with butter, which melted into the bread, and drizzled with condensed milk. There was always a hot flask of jasmine tea to wash it all down. This simple dessert recipe is all about capturing those very simple flavours and variety of textures.

Time: 1 hour + 30 minutes freezing | Makes: 4 servings

ICE CREAM

2 large eggs

2 large egg yolks

½ AUS cup or 104 g or ½ US cup + 1 tsp sugar

1 AUS cup or 250 ml or 1 US cup + 2 tsp thickened cream, cold, divided

⅔ AUS cup or 167 ml or ⅔ US cup + 1½ tsp condensed milk

⅓ AUS cup or 83 ml or ⅓ US cup + ½ tsp very strong jasmine tea

CRUMB

50 g (3½ US tbsp) salted butter

1 AUS cup or 63 g or 1 US cup + 2 tbsp panko

Begin making the ice cream. If using an ice cream churner, pre-chill it now. If not using a churner, see Tip.

Place the eggs, egg yolks and sugar in a large mixing bowl. Whisk until pale and thickened (6 to 8 minutes by hand, 2 to 3 minutes by electric whisk).

Place half of the thickened cream plus all of the condensed milk and jasmine tea in a medium-sized saucepan over medium heat. Bring to a simmer, whisking constantly to fully incorporate the ingredients.

Slowly pour the cream mixture into the eggs, whisking constantly, until fully incorporated. Pour the egg and cream mixture back into the saucepan over low heat. Use a spatula to stir constantly, making sure to scrape the sides and base of the saucepan, for 2 to 3 minutes, or until the mixture is thickened and coats the back of a spoon.

Transfer the mixture back to the large mixing bowl, then add the remaining half of the thickened cream. Whisk thoroughly to combine. Then, pour the mixture into the ice cream churner and churn for 35 to 40 minutes. Place the mixture in the freezer to set further for 30 minutes.

In the meantime, make the crumb: Place a medium-sized frying pan over medium heat. Add the butter and swirl it around the pan. Once the butter begins to brown, add the panko and fry, stirring, for 2 to 3 minutes, or until crispy. Set aside for serving.

Serve scoops of the ice cream with a generous spoonful of crumb sprinkled over the top.

TIP

» If you are not using an ice cream churner, you can still create the ice cream by placing the ice cream mixture in the freezer and whisking it vigorously every 10 to 15 minutes for up to 4 hours, or until set to the consistency you prefer.

PEAR, GINGER + CARDAMOM STRUDEL

In South Asian cuisine (think Bengali, North and South Indian, Pakistani, etc.), some of the more prominent flavours in sweets are cardamom, ginger and semolina. It's a beautiful combination that adds earthiness, nuttiness and natural sweetness. Another very simple dessert to put together, this strudel takes a little bit of preparation and then you pop it in the oven and forget about it until the timer goes off. The spiral of layers of pastry, pears, semolina and that crisp flaky outside are superb. Of course, this needs something tart and creamy to cut through the density and caramel sweetness. South Asian cuisine celebrates and relies on yoghurt, so it only makes sense that a nice big dollop of yoghurt brings this whole dessert together. This is one of those post–Sunday lunch desserts that is best eaten warm.

Time: 1 hour + 10 minutes cooling time | Makes: 4 to 6 servings

PEAR FILLING

25 g (5 tsp) salted butter

3 to 4 large, firm pears, peeled and diced into large cubes (see Tips)

Juice of ½ lemon

1 tsp ground cardamom

1 tsp ground ginger

½ tsp freshly ground black pepper

2 AUS tbsp or 40 g or 2 US tbsp + 2½ tsp dark brown sugar

½ AUS cup or 92 g or ½ US cup + 1 tsp uncooked semolina

PASTRY

6 sheets phyllo pastry

⅓ AUS cup or 83 ml or ⅓ US cup + ½ tsp melted salted butter

SERVING

Plain Greek yoghurt

Preheat the oven to 200°C (400°F). Line a baking tray with baking parchment.

Begin the pear filling: In a large frying pan over medium heat, melt the butter. Then, add the pears, lemon juice, cardamom, ginger, pepper and brown sugar. Stir to combine.

Once the sugar has completely dissolved and the pears are evenly coated, sprinkle the semolina over the pears and mix to combine evenly. Remove from the heat and transfer to a large plate to cool.

In the meantime, place two layers of phyllo pastry on a flat work surface, keeping the remaining phyllo pastry under a damp tea towel to prevent drying. Brush the two layers with melted butter, and repeat with the remaining pastry, adding two layers at a time.

Spread the cooled pear mixture over the buttered pastry, then fold in the sides of the pastry by about 2.5 cm (1 inch). Next, roll the pastry up from bottom to top, like a scroll. Place the strudel on the prepared baking tray and brush the top and sides with more melted butter. Bake for 20 to 30 minutes, or until the pastry is golden brown.

Remove from the oven and allow the strudel to cool for 10 to 15 minutes before slicing with a serrated knife. Serve slices with a big dollop of Greek yoghurt.

TIPS

» Firm, "crunchy" pears are better for baking in this strudel recipe. Use such varieties as Bosc, Anjou or Concorde. Alternatively, use apples.

» This recipe would work with puff pastry, too, but there is no need to butter and layer the pastry. Simply use one sheet of puff pastry, or two with some overlap to make it longer.

YUZU CREPES

Theatre! Magic! That's what you get when you watch the flames erupt in a sunset of blue and orange as the Grand Marnier® gets flambéed in the classic French sweet treat of crêpes Suzette. But more important than the exciting few seconds of theatre is the sweet, caramelised, citrusy flavour emboldened with butter and syrup–drenched crepes. That citrus note is pure pleasure, so in my recipe I've added yuzu, one of the most elegant and unique citrus flavours. It is like walking past the most elegant perfume in an autumn breeze. The distinct taste of lemony-orangey-grapefruity citrus mixed with butter is rich and silky, like a pair of new sheer stockings or a cool silk scarf touching the skin on your neck for the first time. It is sensual and image-provoking in the very best ways, yet all that seems to be on the plate is a few thin pancakes, some caramel and a bit of burnt-off booze. I love the contrast between the complexity of the flavours and the simplicity of this dessert's appearance. It's a little surprising and playful.

Time: 40 minutes | Makes: 12 crepes

CREPES

140 g (5 oz) plain (all-purpose) flour

¼ tsp salt

200 ml (¾ US cup + 2 tsp) whole milk

100 ml (⅓ US cup + 4 tsp) water

2 large eggs

25 g (5 tsp) salted butter, melted, plus a little more for pan

FILLING

3 AUS tbsp or 60 g or 4 US tbsp caster (superfine) sugar

200 ml (¾ US cup + 2 tsp) fresh orange juice (from 2 to 3 oranges)

50 ml (3 US tbsp + 1 tsp) yuzu juice

Zest of 1 yuzu or lemon

1 AUS tbsp or 20 ml or 4 tsp honey

1 AUS tbsp or 20 ml or 4 tsp Grand Marnier or Cointreau (optional)

50 g (3½ US tbsp) salted butter

SERVING

Crème fraîche

Begin with making the crepes: Sift the flour and salt into a medium-sized mixing bowl and make a well in the middle. Add the milk, water, eggs and melted butter to the well and whisk until a smooth, fully incorporated, slightly runny batter is formed. Let the batter rest for 15 minutes.

Heat a medium-sized non-stick frying pan over medium heat. Lightly grease the pan with melted butter. Stir the crepe batter well before pouring 2 to 3 AUS table-spoons (40 to 60 ml or 2 US tablespoons + 2 teaspoons to ¼ US cup) of the batter into the pan and swirling it to coat the bottom of the pan evenly and completely. It should be a very thin layer of batter. Cook the crepe for about 45 seconds on one side until golden, then use a palette knife or spatula to flip the crepe to the other side and cook for another 30 to 40 seconds.

Transfer the cooked crepe to a plate. Repeat the cooking process with all the remaining batter.

Once the crepes have been cooked, keep the frying pan over medium heat. Add the caster sugar and let it caramelise into an amber colour. Then, turn off the heat and immediately and carefully add the orange juice, yuzu juice, zest and honey. Whisk the mixture well, then turn the heat back on to medium.

Add the Grand Marnier. At this point, you could flambé the mixture to burn off the alcohol, or simply bring it up to a simmer. Once simmering, whisk in the butter, a bit at a time, then lower the heat as low as possible to keep the sauce warm.

Fold the crepes into quarters, dip them in the sauce and plate three crepes per serving. Once all the crepes are plated, divide and pour any leftover sauce over the crepes. Serve with a dollop of cold crème fraîche.

TIP

» The crepe batter can be made a day in advance and kept covered in the fridge. Simply stir well before cooking.

SNACKS + SIDES

These are the recipes that are made for grazing, snacking and filling the table. From picnic powerhouse recipes to stunning side dishes, the recipes in this chapter represent my favourite textures and morsels. When I envisioned this chapter, I thought of the moments of biting into the perfect picnic sandwich, generously filled with soft textures contrasted with crisp crunch; and the accompaniments to a meal that end up being the conversation piece; the crispiest potatoes with bold, sticky sauces, and all the extra salty, rich, buttery, sharp, tangy, herby, flavours that accentuate the best bites of food. You won't find your regular peanut butter sandwiches in this chapter. Instead, these recipes are creative spins on classic Asian comfort foods and market stall treats.

CRISPY HONEY GARLIC ROAST POTATOES

What makes a good roast dinner? I'd say it is as dependent on a succulent slice of good quality, tender meat as the sides that accompany it. Mum used to lay a bed of carrots, potatoes, pumpkin, whole garlic bulbs and chunky zucchini seasoned lightly with honey and Chinese five-spice powder under a roast pork shoulder. The potatoes were never crispy, they were always fluffy, soft and a little on the greasy side. But the flavour of five-spice and honey with the potatoes is what made my heart sing. Then, I learnt how to make crispy potatoes and it just made sense to take those dreamy potatoes to the next level. Try these crispy, lightly sweet and aromatic potatoes and your heart will sing along with mine.

Time: 90 minutes | Makes: 4 servings

600 g (21 oz) high-starch potatoes, skin on, washed (see Tips)

Salt

4 AUS tbsp or 80 ml or ⅓ US cup neutral oil (rice bran, grapeseed, vegetable)

3 cloves garlic, finely minced or grated

1 AUS tbsp or 8 g or 4 tsp Chinese five-spice powder

2 to 3 AUS tbsp or 60 to 80 ml or ¼ to ⅓ US cup honey

Salt, to taste

SERVING

2 AUS tbsp or 8 g or 2 US tbsp + 2 tsp finely sliced fresh chives

Preheat the oven to 220°C (425°F).

Slice the potatoes into quarters (or halves for smaller potatoes, roughly 4- to 5-cm [1½- to 2-inch] pieces) and rinse twice under cold water to remove any excess starch. Then, place the potatoes in a large pot, cover them with cold water and add two generous pinches of salt. Bring the potatoes to a boil and allow them to boil for 10 to 12 minutes, or until fork-tender.

Drain the potatoes in a colander or sieve, and once the water has been drained off, shake the colander or sieve to scuff the surfaces of the potato. Then, place the potatoes on a wire rack over a tray or tea towel to cool completely; this may take approximately 15 minutes.

While the potatoes are cooling, pour the oil into a large roasting tray and place it in the oven to preheat for 10 minutes. Once the oil is very hot and the potatoes are cold, carefully add the potatoes to the oil. Roast for 50 minutes to 1 hour, shaking the tray and turning over the potatoes halfway through.

While the potatoes roast, mix together the garlic, five-spice powder and honey in a small bowl until well combined. Once the potatoes are roasted and crispy, remove the tray from the oven and drizzle the honey mixture all over the potatoes while still hot. Toss the potatoes to coat evenly. Season with a sprinkling of salt to taste.

Transfer the potatoes to your serving plate and garnish with chives.

TIPS

» High-starch potatoes (Maris Piper, King Edward, russet, Burbank varieties) produce a "fluffier" interior while being able to hold a crisp outer layer and are better suited to roasting.

» The potatoes must be cooled completely before roasting, otherwise the moisture from warm potatoes will create steam and make soggy, greasy potatoes.

» Your oven must be preheated, and the oil must be preheated before adding the cold potatoes in order to achieve maximum crispiness.

TAIWANESE POPCORN CHICKEN

During my years at Mandarin school, flocks of students would flow into the hallways during the lunch break to be met with the smell of sweet baked breads and cakes, and fried chicken. A group of mothers set up trestle tables, stacking pastries and buns into tall piles, and fishing out fried chicken drumsticks with the most aromatic batter of Szechuan peppercorns and Chinese five-spice onto wire racks. I didn't really fit in with my own peers, so lunch times were spent going to my brother's classroom and hanging out with his friends who seemed much nicer to me. As a treat, my brother would buy me lunch. The fried chicken always made me feel better. This recipe captures the aroma and juiciness of those comforting lunches. The special thing about this recipe is that it uses glutinous rice flour instead of other starches. This gives far better "beading" of the batter, which allows for tiny crunchy pearls to form for that signature Taiwanese fried chicken look.

Time: 45 minutes | Makes: 4 servings

680 g (1½ lb) chicken thighs, cut into uniform bite-sized pieces

MARINADE

1 AUS tbsp or 20 ml or 4 tsp light soy sauce

3 AUS tbsp or 60 ml or ¼ US cup oyster sauce

1 large egg white

½ tsp salt

½ tsp freshly ground black pepper

6 g (2 tsp) garlic powder

1 tsp ground white pepper

1 tsp ground Szechuan peppercorns

1 tsp Chinese five-spice powder

½ tsp sugar

FOR FRYING

Enough oil to reach a depth of 2.5 to 5 cm (1" to 2") in a saucepan or frying pan

1 AUS cup or 155 g or 1 US cup + ½ US tbsp glutinous rice flour

8 AUS tbsp or 160 ml or ⅔ US cup water

1 AUS cup or 42 g or 1 US cup + ½ US tbsp fresh Thai basil leaves

Place the chicken pieces and marinade ingredients in a bowl. Mix thoroughly, massaging the marinade into the chicken pieces. Set aside for 15 minutes.

In the meantime, heat the oil for frying to 165°C (330°F).

Before frying, place the glutinous rice flour in a large bowl. Add 1 or 2 AUS tablespoons (20 ml or 4 teaspoons per tablespoon) of water at a time, mixing in between additions to create small lumps. Break any larger lumps into smaller lumps. Add a few pieces of the chicken to the glutinous rice flour mixture and mix until evenly coated. Add extra spoonfuls of glutinous rice flour, if needed, to completely coat the chicken.

Fry the chicken in small batches (four or five pieces at a time) for 2 to 3 minutes, or until lightly golden brown. Then, remove the chicken and set it on a wire rack over a tray to rest. Continue with the remaining chicken.

Increase the heat of the frying oil to 190°C (375°). Re-fry the fried batches of chicken for 1 to 2 minutes and set aside to rest on the rack again. Then, fry the Thai basil leaves for about 20 to 30 seconds, just until they become translucent and crispy.

Serve the popcorn chicken with the Thai basil leaves scattered over the top.

TIPS

» Generally, if you put a wooden chopstick or handle of a wooden spoon into the oil and it actively bubbles, the oil is hot enough to fry. If there is no bubbling or very little bubbling, the oil is not hot enough.

» Don't be scared to "over-use" the glutinous rice flour. You want to make sure the flour is lumpy and gets in all the nooks and crannies of the chicken.

» The Thai basil leaves may be replaced with regular basil leaves.

CHARSIU SANGA

(Sandwich)

Family days at the beach were rare given my mother worked seven days a week for years. When December and January rolled around and summer was at its peak heat, we were lucky enough to enjoy several public holidays in a row. It meant packing a cooler bag full of treats and heading to the coast. My mother would pack leftovers from the dinner before, sometimes stuffing them into bread or wraps, and cold fruit salad. The best sandwiches were stuffed with Chinese barbecue pork (charsiu) and crisp cabbage with just a smidge of Japanese mayonnaise.

Time: 40 minutes | Makes: 4 servings

CHARSIU

4 AUS tbsp or 80 ml or ⅓ US cup hoisin sauce

4 g (2 tsp) Chinese five-spice powder

5 to 10 ml (1 to 2 tsp) honey

½ tsp ground white pepper

2 AUS tbsp or 40 ml or 2 US tbsp + 2 tsp light soy sauce

1 AUS tbsp or 20 ml or 4 tsp neutral oil

750 to 800 g (26.5 to 28 oz) pork belly rashers; remove skin

SALAD

1½ AUS cups or 100 g or 3.5 oz very finely shredded cabbage (green or purple or a mixture according to your preference)

1 AUS cup loosely packed or 16 g or 1 US cup fresh coriander (cilantro) leaves

1½ AUS tbsp or 30 ml or 2 US tbsp Kewpie Mayonnaise (or other Japanese mayonnaise)

2 AUS tbsp or 40 ml or 2 US tbsp + 2 tsp Garlic Sauce (page 23; optional)

8 thick slices Japanese milk bread (or other very soft bread)

For the charsiu, mix together all the charsiu ingredients, except the pork belly, in a bowl until fully incorporated. Then, add the pork belly, mixing to coat. Leave to marinate for 10 to 15 minutes (or up to an hour), or overnight covered in the fridge.

Grill or broil the pork belly on a rack over a lined tray at middle height, not too close to the grill. Grill for 5 minutes per side until dark, caramelised and lightly charred. Alternatively, pan-fry over medium heat for 3 to 4 minutes each side. Remove from the heat and let rest for 5 minutes before slicing.

In the meantime, for the salad, mix together the cabbage, coriander leaves and Kewpie together in a medium-sized bowl and set aside.

If using, spread a thin layer, approximately a teaspoon, of garlic sauce on each slice of bread. Layer a small handful of the salad to a slice of bread, then add a generous layer of charsiu, then top with another slice of bread. Slice each sandwich into two rectangular halves.

TIP

» If you ever have leftover charsiu from a takeout night, save it for these types of sandwiches!

MA LA (SPICY + NUMBING) EGGPLANT TOASTS

"I'm so ready to come home now," I'd text a couple days before my long work trips or vacations ended.

"See you soon 🥢. What do you want to eat?" Mum would reply almost immediately, as if she had been waiting for my text all day.

"Pork bone soup and black eggplant please," I'd respond almost immediately, as if I had been thinking of the meal for days on end.

"Of course, I already bought the eggplants 🍆," Mum would say.

One of my favourite dishes my Mum made was what I called "black eggplant." It's a chunky, mushy dish of eggplant that has been braised in dark soy sauce and black vinegar to make it as black as midnight and then served with celery leaves stirred through at the end. It sounds frightening, but it tastes magical. When it's eaten with hot steamed rice, it touches your soul somehow. It is one dish that makes me think of Mum and all the times she would make it for me as a "welcome home" dish. It is as comforting to me as one of her hugs. This snack recipe is inspired by "black eggplant" and the fullness of flavour and savouriness.

Time: 30 minutes | Makes: 4 servings

3 g (2 tsp) Szechuan peppercorns

1 tsp fennel seeds

2 AUS tbsp or 40 ml or 2 US tbsp + 2 tsp neutral oil (grapeseed, rice bran, canola, etc.)

4 cloves garlic, finely chopped

1 globe eggplant, halved lengthways and sliced into roughly 3-mm (⅛") slices

2 AUS tbsp or 40 ml or 2 US tbsp + 2 tsp Chinkiang black vinegar

½ AUS tbsp or 10 ml or 2 tsp light soy sauce

2 AUS tbsp or 40 ml or 2 US tbsp + 2 tsp Lao Gan Ma Crispy Chilli Oil

12 pieces brioche, 8 x 4 cm (3⅜" x 1½"), toasted

SERVING

Celery leaves

In a small, dry frying pan over medium heat, toast the Szechuan peppercorns and fennel seeds, tossing or stirring intermittently, for 2 to 3 minutes, or until fragrant and darkened slightly. Once toasted, remove from the heat and allow to cool for 10 minutes before finely grinding in a mortar and pestle or spice grinder, or chopping with a knife.

In a large frying pan or wok over medium-high heat, heat the neutral oil. Once hot, stir-fry the garlic for 10 seconds, then add the eggplant. Increase the heat to high. Stir-fry the eggplant for 2 to 3 minutes, or until starting to colour. Add the Szechuan peppercorns, fennel seeds, black vinegar and soy sauce. Stir-fry for another 2 to 3 minutes, or until the liquid has mostly evaporated.

Add the Lao Gan Ma Crispy Chilli Oil and stir-fry for another 1 to 2 minutes to evenly disperse. Then, transfer the eggplant to a dish, leaving any liquid behind. Top each toast generously with the eggplant. Garnish with celery leaves.

TIPS

» The thinner you cut the eggplant, the quicker they will cook.

» You could cut the eggplant a few hours ahead of serving; just place the slices in salted cold water in the fridge so they don't discolour or become bitter.

CRISPY TOFU BITES WITH PONZU

A delicate crispy shell surrounding a silky-smooth centre. That's the beauty of these crispy tofu bites. It's all about satisfying little bites with a solid hit of salt, chilli and fragrant spices. In this recipe, I've blended my brother's favourite fried tofu dishes together: fried salt and pepper tofu and Agedashi tofu, which typically sits in a soy-based sauce like ponzu. For my brother, it's all about the texture and making sure there's enough flavour to be carried by the neutral tofu. Fried tofu of any kind is a crowd-pleaser and definitely a comfort food for my brother and me. You've got to eat these right away after frying so they're crispy and hot all the way through.

Time: 20 to 30 minutes | Makes: 4 servings

TOFU BITES

1 (500-g [shy 18-oz]) package medium-firm tofu, drained well and cut into bite-sized cubes

1½ AUS cups or 200 g or 1½ US cups + 1 US tbsp tapioca starch

1 tsp ground white pepper

1 AUS tbsp or 8 g or 4 tsp Chinese five-spice powder

6 g (1 tsp) salt

Vegetable oil, for frying

SEASONING

1 AUS tbsp or 12 g or 1½ tbsp garlic powder

1 AUS tbsp or 9 g or 4 tsp onion powder

4 g (2 tsp) shichimi togarashi (Japanese seven-spice powder)

½ tsp salt

SERVING

Ponzu (page 24)

Drain the tofu well and leave for 10 minutes on a thick layer of paper towels, rotating occasionally to soak up excess moisture. In a large mixing bowl, mix together the tapioca starch, white pepper, Chinese five-spice powder and salt. Whisk until evenly combined.

Drop the pieces of tofu into the tapioca starch mixture and toss until all the pieces are coated.

Heat the frying oil in a large skillet over medium-high heat. Once the oil is hot, carefully add the tofu pieces and fry for 1 to 2 minutes per side, or until crispy and bubbly. Transfer the tofu pieces to a rack over a tray to drain.

Increase the heat of the frying oil to high. Once the oil is hot again, add the tofu pieces back, frying for 30 seconds to a minute per side, or until lightly golden brown. Note that tapioca starch does not brown deeply like other starches. Remove the tofu and drain on the rack again. Turn off the heat.

Mix together all the seasoning ingredients in a large mixing bowl. Then, toss the hot, crispy tofu through the seasoning to coat. Serve immediately with Ponzu.

LAP CHEONG OMELETTE BREAKFAST SANDWICHES

I probably consumed at least two or three of these Chinese sausage (lap cheong) and egg sandwiches a week during my final year of high school and again in my first year of full-time work. It was my mother's way of making sure I started the day right and was taking care of myself. These are extraordinarily simple and my favourite part about them is the sweet crispy bits of sausage caught in creamy, slightly runny curds of egg, which is cut with the tang of tomato sauce (ketchup). It's the Chinese version of a sausage and egg breakfast sandwich. Honestly, I've also made these for quick, can't-be-bothered-to-do-much dinners, too.

Time: 10 minutes | Makes: 4 servings

2 AUS tbsp or 40 ml or 2 US tbsp + 2 tsp neutral oil (rice bran, grapeseed, vegetable)

3 lap cheong sausages (total weight approximately 100 g [3.5 oz]), finely sliced

1 tsp salt

½ tsp freshly ground black pepper

8 large eggs, cracked into a bowl

8 slices white sandwich bread, toasted and buttered

SERVING

Tomato sauce (ketchup)

In a large frying pan over medium high heat, heat the oil. Once the oil is hot, add the sliced lap cheong and stir-fry for 30 to 40 seconds, or until starting to colour.

Thoroughly beat the salt and pepper into the eggs. Then, pour the egg mixture into the pan, using a fork or spatula to immediately start scrambling the eggs and mixing them thoroughly with the lap cheong. After about 10 seconds, turn off the heat and stop scrambling the eggs once everything has come together in one solid mass. The residual heat will continue cooking the eggs.

After about 30 to 40 seconds, while the top of the omelette is still shiny and a little runny, divide the omelette into four portions and lay each portion between two pieces of buttered toast. Top each omelette with tomato sauce and serve the sandwiches whole or sliced in half.

TIPS

» Adding a handful of sautéed, sliced brown onion before the lap cheong adds a completely different dimension of flavour.

» If you prefer your egg to be cooked all the way through, simply flip the omelette and cook for a few more seconds before serving.

PRAWN CUTLETS AND TARTAR SAUCE

Crunchy, golden and shaped like a curled fan, these prawns are super tender and moist on the inside. I have a weakness for fried snacks. Knowing this, Mum would make these prawn cutlets, fried wontons and spring rolls for special occasions like Chinese New Year, birthdays and Christmas. This recipe is a sure way to spread joy. I also have to admit that the tartar sauce recipe I've included is brilliant. I use it on everything from tacos to burgers, a little dippy dip for fried goodness and also fresh veggie crudités. It's the mixture of dill, mustard, celery and salty capers amongst everything else that really packs a punch.

Time: 20 minutes | Makes: 4 servings

PRAWNS

Enough oil for frying to reach a depth of 2.5 to 5 cm (1" to 2") in a saucepan or frying pan

16 large raw prawns (shrimp), peeled with tail on

1 AUS cup or 130 g or 1 US cup + 2 tsp plain (all-purpose) flour

1 large egg, beaten

1 tsp salt

1 tsp freshly ground black pepper

1 AUS cup or 63 g or 1 US cup + 2 tbsp panko

TARTAR SAUCE

1 AUS cup or 250 ml or 1 US cup + 2 tsp mayonnaise

Juice of 1 lemon

90 g (3 oz) cornichons, finely chopped

2 AUS tbsp or 23 g or 2 US tbsp + 2 tsp baby capers, drained, finely chopped

½ red onion, finely diced

10 g (0.5 oz) fresh dill fronds, finely chopped

20 g (0.75 oz) fresh flat-leaf parsley, finely chopped

10 g (0.5 oz) celery leaves, finely chopped

1 AUS tbsp or 20 ml or 4 tsp whole-grain mustard

Salt and freshly ground black pepper

SERVING

Lemon wedges

Heat the oil to 170°C (325°F).

Butterfly each prawn without slicing all the way through.

Place the flour in a bowl. Liberally season the flour and, separately, the beaten egg with salt and pepper. Place the panko in a third bowl.

Coat each prawn with the seasoned flour, then dip them in the egg mixture, then coat them in panko. Set aside on a plate.

Fry three or four prawns at a time for 2 to 3 minutes, or until golden brown, flipping halfway during frying. Set the fried prawns on a rack over a tray while you continue to fry the rest in batches. Season the prawns lightly with salt as they come out of the oil.

For the tartar sauce, in a small bowl, combine all the sauce ingredients and mix well. Serve the prawns with the tartar sauce and lemon wedges.

SWEET + SPICY CRISPY ANCHOVIES (IKAN BILIS) AND PEANUTS

I'd argue that the most popular snacks in Southeast Asia are the perfect combination of sweetness, saltiness, spiciness and texture. Snacks don't stop at potato chips and chocolate bars. The snack aisles are lined with dried fish, squid, meat jerky, braised and preserved meats and eggs, widening the whole spectrum of what can be considered a "snack." Not only are there a huge variety of combinations of flavours, but snacks are more satisfying and interesting in texture and appearance than their Western counterparts. These clusters of fried anchovies and peanuts are a perfect example. Mum would make a big batch of these sticky morsels and keep them in an airtight jar. Whenever we had guests over or enjoyed a Sunday afternoon cup of tea, a little plate of these would appear, bringing a little extra joy to the day. You could also serve them as a crispy and crunchy topper to salads, or as a side dish to eat with grilled meats and vegetables.

Time: 30 minutes | Makes: 4 servings

½ AUS cup or 78 g or ½ US cup skinless, unsalted peanuts

50 g (2 oz) dried ikan bilis (anchovies)

3 AUS tbsp or 60 ml or ¼ US cup vegetable oil

3 AUS tbsp or 60 ml or ¼ US cup ABC Chilli Sauce (see page 17) or other chilli sauce

1 AUS tbsp or 20 g or 4 tsp dark brown sugar

3 AUS tbsp or 60 ml or ¼ US cup vinegar

½ tsp salt

1 to 2 AUS tbsp or 11 to 21 g or 4 tsp to 2 US tbsp + 1 tsp toasted white sesame seeds

Roast the peanuts in a 180°C (350°F) oven for 6 to 8 minutes, or until lightly browned. Remove from the oven and set aside. In the meantime, rinse the anchovies in cold water and then drain well. Use paper towels to pat dry.

In a large frying pan over low heat, heat the oil and fry the anchovies for 8 to 10 minutes, or until golden brown. Remove the anchovies and set aside, reserving the oil in the pan.

In the same pan over medium heat, add the ABC Chilli Sauce, brown sugar, vinegar and salt. Stir thoroughly and allow to simmer and reduce for 2 to 3 minutes, or until thickened. Then, add the crispy anchovies, peanuts and sesame seeds to the sauce. Mix well to coat evenly. Remove from the heat and allow to cool and crisp up on a plate or tray.

TIPS

» Gochujang can be used instead of chilli sauce for a slightly sweeter flavour and deeper red colour.

» The brown sugar can be replaced with your preferred sugar.

» You could add crispy tempeh or other nuts and seeds.

"Pancakes!" Mum exclaimed, placing down a plate of very brown jagged patties of fried something on the table. The edge of the plate glistened with a greasy thumbprint. I stared cautiously at the brown, spidery "pancakes."

"Veggie. Like the Korean pancakes." Mum was referring to the various delicious *jeon* you commonly find in Korean street food stalls or grocery stores. They're a mixture of vegetables and protein smothered in an eggy batter and then pan-fried until they're crispy around the edges and pillowy in the middle.

I picked one up, dipped it in Maggi Seasoning and ate it. The vegetables were still raw and the batter was basically just egg.

"Not nice?" Mum was watching my face closely.

"Are the potatoes meant to be crunchy?"

POTATO AND ZUCCHINI CROQUETTES
with Garlic Sauce

Mum's third and fourth attempts the next week were far better, and she eventually did master her version of jeon.

This recipe avoids all manner of raw potatoes, but still adds texture with the zucchini. By pre-cooking and mashing the potatoes, you get this delicious, hearty, cakey texture. Using Maggi Seasoning in the actual potatoes means you get that umami with each bite.

Time: 45 minutes | Makes: 4 servings (10 to 12 croquettes)

300 g (10.5 oz) washed potatoes, peeled and halved

Salt

400 g (14 oz) zucchini, coarsely grated

4 spring onions (scallions), finely chopped

⅔ AUS cup or 90 g or shy ¾ US cup plain (all-purpose) flour

2 AUS tbsp or 40 ml or 2 US tbsp + 2 tsp Maggi Seasoning (optional)

9 g (1½ tsp) salt (optional)

1 tsp freshly ground black pepper (optional)

Neutral oil, for shallow-frying

SERVING

Garlic Sauce (page 23)

Place the potatoes in a small saucepan, cover with water, add about 1 AUS tablespoon (24 g or 4 teaspoons) of salt and bring to a boil over medium-high heat. Cook until tender, approximately 15 to 18 minutes. Drain the water from the saucepan, return the potatoes to the pan and coarsely mash with a potato masher or fork.

In the meantime, place the grated zucchini in a clean tea towel and squeeze very firmly over the sink to remove as much moisture as possible. Transfer the zucchini to the mashed potato mixture, along with the spring onions and flour. Season with Maggi Seasoning (if using), or 1½ teaspoons (9 g) of salt plus 1 teaspoon of pepper, and mix well to combine.

Heat 2.5 cm (1 inch) of oil in a large frying pan over medium-high heat. Roughly divide the mixture into 10 to 12 portions and shape each portion into an oval croquette. Fry the croquettes in batches for about 6 minutes, or until golden and crisp, flipping them over halfway through cooking. Remove with a slotted spoon and drain on a rack over a tray.

Serve the croquettes with garlic sauce.

SPICED LAMB AND PEAS ON BRIOCHE TOASTS

Lamb is a loved protein in our household and popular amongst most Australian families. We grew up eating roast lamb with rosemary and garlic, and on the odd occasion, Mum would make *rogan josh* (Kashmiri lamb) or a hearty stew. I loved the gamey roundness of the flavour of lamb, the texture of the tender slow-cooked roast shoulder and the way it danced perfectly with the spices. Naughtily, my favourite morsels were actually the next-morning leftovers, the lamb still fridge-cold but the South Asian spices still tingly and warming on my tongue. It was the perfect sneaky bite to wake up my appetite for the day. It wasn't actually until I was in my early twenties that I tasted raw lamb in the form of kibbeh at a Middle Eastern restaurant. It excited me and immediately drew me back into those mornings standing in the fridge doorway, picking at the leftover roast lamb. This lamb tartare is a sexy little canapé to serve and brings me as much satisfaction as those morning memories.

Time: 25 minutes | Makes: 4 servings

SPICE MIX

1 tsp medium-hot red chilli powder

1 tsp ground ginger

1 AUS tbsp or 8 g or 4 tsp ground coriander seeds

1 tsp ground cumin

½ tsp ground cloves

1 tsp ground cardamom

6 g (2 tsp) garlic powder

5 g (2 tsp) onion powder

½ tsp ground white pepper

9 g (1½ tsp) salt

250 g (9 oz) fresh lamb backstrap (also called eye of loin)

1 AUS tbsp or 20 ml or 4 tsp sesame oil

In a medium-sized mixing bowl, combine all the ingredients for the spice mix and whisk thoroughly.

Slice the backstrap into 5-mm (scant ¼-inch) cubes and add to the bowl of spices. Stir thoroughly to coat evenly. Add the sesame oil and stir again to coat. Set the lamb mixture aside in the fridge to chill for 10 to 15 minutes.

(continued)

PEA PURÉE

2 AUS cups or 500 ml or 2 US cups + 2 US tbsp water

1 AUS cup or 135 g or 1 US cup + 2 tsp frozen peas

2 bay leaves

12 g (2 tsp) salt

40 g (2 US tbsp + 2½ tsp) salted butter

Neutral oil, for frying

1 to 2 brioche hot dog buns, sliced into 5 mm (scant ¼") toasts

Salt

SERVING

Garlic Sauce (page 23)

Fresh peas (larger peas sliced in half)

Fresh shiso leaves, finely sliced

For the pea purée, bring the water to a boil in a small saucepan over medium-high heat. Add the peas, bay leaves and salt. Boil for 5 to 6 minutes. Remove the bay leaves, then place 2 AUS tablespoons (40 ml or 2 US tablespoons + 2 teaspoons) of the pea boiling water in a blender along with the drained peas and salted butter. Blitz until smooth. Transfer the purée to a squeeze bottle or have ready a small spoon.

Heat a small saucepan of neutral oil over medium heat. Once hot, fry 2 or 3 slices of the brioche at a time for 1 to 2 minutes, or until golden brown. Drain on paper towels and season with salt while still hot. Repeat with the remaining slices of brioche.

To assemble, place the Garlic Sauce in a separate squeeze bottle and squeeze a peanut-sized dollop of it onto one end of the brioche toast. Alternatively, use a small spoon. Squeeze or spoon an equal amount of the pea purée next to the garlic sauce. Then, top the sauces with a heaped teaspoon of the lamb tartare. Garnish with fresh peas and finely sliced shiso.

PALAK
PANEER DIP

"I found a recipe on the Google that looks really good!" Mum was digging through one of the cupboards looking for a sieve. It was 2005 and "the Google" was her latest discovery after my brother showed her how to open an internet browser and search for anything she could possibly imagine. Finally pulling out a sieve, Mum launched into making her very own paneer (soft cheese). Then, she whipped out a bunch of spinach and spices. Soon, the whole kitchen smelled of warm cumin and garlic. When the finished dish landed on the table, it was a big bowl of dark green chunky soup. My brother and I were a little alarmed. We love Indian cuisine, but at the time, all we knew was "butter chicken" and "lamb korma" from the Indian restaurant down the road. The paneer was watery and falling apart. We scooped a little onto our rice, and after the first taste, we were sold. It was rich and light at the same time. The bitter, mustardy fenugreek and sweet coriander perfectly matched the minerally spinach! We finished off the whole bowl. At the end of the meal, my brother leant back in his chair, his full tummy poking out a little, and said, "I've never eaten cheese on rice before. I wish I had some naan to mop up the bowl." Well, this recipe solves the problem; it is thick, creamy, full of spice and perfect with naan.

Time: 1 hour | Makes: 4 servings

PANEER

2 L (8½ US cups) full-fat milk

5 AUS tbsp or 100 ml or ⅓ US cup + 4 tsp fresh lemon juice or white vinegar

PALAK PANEER

30 g (6½ tsp) ghee (clarified butter) or unsalted full-fat butter

2 brown or yellow onions, finely chopped

1 tsp whole fenugreek seeds

1 tsp ground cumin

1 tsp ground coriander

¾ tsp kosher salt (if using table salt, reduce by ¼ tsp)

¼ tsp freshly ground black pepper

4 cloves garlic, finely chopped

4 g (2 tsp) finely grated fresh ginger

2 Roma or Gourmet tomatoes, peeled, seeded and diced

2 green cayenne or serrano chillies

¼ AUS cup or 63 ml or ¼ US cup + ½ tsp water

In a large saucepan over medium heat, warm the milk until just before it begins to boil. The top of the milk should look foamy and steam should be rising from the surface.

Turn off the heat and add the lemon juice to the milk. Stir thoroughly for 50 to 60 seconds with a spatula, making sure to scrape the bottom and sides of the saucepan. Leave the milk to curdle (the solids will separate from the liquid whey [see Tips]). These curdled solids are the paneer.

Place a strainer or colander over a large bowl and line the strainer with two or three layers of cheesecloth. Strain the paneer through the cloth. Use the spatula to press down gently on the paneer to squeeze out more whey. Then, cover the top of the paneer with the overhanging cheesecloth or another layer. Place some clean tins or a heavy saucepan on the top to press the paneer further and remove excess moisture. Set aside for 15 to 20 minutes.

In the meantime, make the palak paneer. Melt the ghee in a large pot over medium-high heat, then sauté the onions, fenugreek, cumin, coriander, salt and black pepper for 3 to 4 minutes, or until fragrant and the onions have softened. Add the garlic and ginger and continue to sauté for 2 to 3 minutes, or until the garlic browns. Add the tomato, chillies and water and sauté for a further 2 to 3 minutes, or until softened and well combined.

(continued)

700 g (24.5 oz) fresh English spinach leaves, washed and roughly chopped

1 AUS tbsp or 20 ml or 4 tsp fresh lemon juice

⅓ AUS cup or 83 ml or ⅓ US cup + ½ tsp heavy cream

SERVING

Sliced green cayenne or serrano chillies

Toasted naan

Lower the heat to medium and add about half of the spinach, or however much you can fit in the pot, and sauté until it is completely wilted. Repeat this step until all the spinach has been incorporated. Allow to cook, stirring occasionally, for 5 minutes, or until fully softened and combined.

Turn off the heat, then add the lemon juice, stir well to incorporate, then add the cream, mixing well. Transfer the mixture to a blender and blend until smooth. Set aside until cool.

Remove the paneer from the cheesecloth and transfer it to a medium-sized mixing bowl. Add a generous pinch of salt and mix well. The mixture should be thick but spreadable.

Transfer the seasoned paneer to a serving bowl. Add a few dollops of the palak paneer and use a spoon to swirl the green mixture through the paneer. Garnish with sliced green chillies and serve with warm, toasted naan.

TIPS

» If the milk doesn't curdle at first when making the paneer, turn the stove back on and bring back to a gentle boil until the solids separate, then turn off the stove.

» If the paneer is too soft to handle, allow it to drain for a further 10 to 15 minutes. If the paneer is too firm, mix in a tablespoon of heavy cream at a time until it reaches your preferred consistency.

» Paneer can be stored in a clean, airtight container in the fridge for 3 to 4 days.

» Palak paneer needs to be made with fully grown spinach. English spinach gives the best flavour. Frozen spinach may be used, but it should be de-frosted, squeezed to remove excess moisture and doubled or tripled in quantity.

GARLIC ANCHOVY FLATBREADS

Anchovies always featured in the food I ate while growing up and were always stored in airtight containers in the fridge. Usually, they were weird-looking skeletal things, dried and added to soups to boost seafood flavours and umami, or fried until crispy to add texture and saltiness to dishes. They were also usually very small fish. When I discovered Spanish anchovies for the first time, I saw plump, long, blushing fillets sealed in tiny glass jars and little tins brimming with oil. Then, I tried them. It was biblical. It was like rediscovering the power of salt and MSG all in one. The flavour blew me away, the texture of the soft fillets melted in the warmth of my mouth and the oil was like silky oceanic sheets. It only gets better with the pairing of garlic and hot, freshly baked bread with a little charring.

Time: 1½ to 2 hours | Makes: 12 pieces

DOUGH

10 g (2½ tsp) instant dried yeast

100 ml (⅓ US cup + 4 tsp) water, slightly warm

1 tsp sugar

500 g (17.5 oz) strong white bread flour, plus more for dusting

9 g (1½ tsp) salt

300 ml (1¼ US cups + 1 tsp) water, at room temperature, divided

50 g (3½ US tbsp) unsalted butter

GARLIC BUTTER

100 g (7 tbsp) unsalted butter, softened

3 cloves garlic, minced

½ tsp salt

SERVING

48 anchovy fillets, packed in oil (best quality you can find)

Salt flakes

Lao Gan Ma Crispy Chilli Oil (optional)

For the dough, combine the yeast, warm water and sugar in a medium-sized pitcher or bowl. Stir well and set aside for 30 minutes, until very frothy.

In a large mixing bowl or the bowl of a stand mixer, stir together the bread flour and salt. Once combined, add the yeast mixture, two-thirds of the room-temperature water and the butter. Then, use your hands or a dough hook on the stand mixer to mix the dough ingredients together, until combined. Gradually add the remaining third of the room-temperature water as you continue to mix.

Knead for 10 to 12 minutes by hand, or for 6 to 8 minutes using the stand mixer, until a smooth dough forms. Then, cover the dough in the bowl with a clean tea towel or loosely with cling film (plastic wrap) and leave in a warm place to rise for 1 to 2 hours, or in the fridge overnight, until it has doubled in size.

Preheat the oven to 250 to 260°C (480 to 500°F) or as hot as the oven will go, and place a large, dry baking tray in the oven to heat. Place the dough on a lightly floured surface and knead gently for 1 to 2 minutes to knock out the air. Then, divide the dough into 12 equal pieces. Form each piece into a smooth ball and set aside for 15 minutes.

In the meantime, mix together the butter, garlic and salt in a small bowl to make the garlic butter.

On a lightly floured surface, roll out each dough ball into roughly 3-mm (⅛-inch)-thick rounds. Dust both sides of the dough lightly with flour, then carefully transfer one or two of rounds at a time to the hot tray in the oven. Bake for 5 to 6 minutes, or until blackened blisters appear and the dough has puffed up. Remove the cooked breads from the tray and immediately brush with garlic butter and dress with three to four anchovy fillets and a generous sprinkle of flaky salt.

Drizzle a little Lao Gan Ma Crispy Chilli Oil over the top, if you wish. Repeat with all the remaining dough portions and serve hot.

DAMPER WITH CORIANDER SEED HONEY AND BUTTER

When fifth grade camp rolled around, I was distraught. I hadn't spent many nights away from my family and I was very particular about my night-time routines and my familiar space. I remember crying for a couple of nights before I was due to leave for the Bathurst Goldfields. It's an iconic excursion destination for primary school students. My mother climbed into bed with me and cuddled me close. She made it a point to tell me that I would be having more of these experiences away from home and, while they may feel distressing, I should think of one positive thing to look forward to on each trip. Mum described to me the itinerary and comfortingly said, "There's a camp cookout one night! You'll learn to make damper. Did you know that's one of the first Australian breads I tried when I came to Sydney? You can teach me the recipe when you get home." Sure enough, the cookout came to pass and I had an amazing time making my own damper (a historically significant unleavened bread baked over fire in Australia). We wrapped the dough around a stick and cooked it over the fire and ate it warm with salty butter and runny honey. It filled my belly with comfort, reassurance and security. The memory has stayed with me since and it isn't lost on me that the only new friend I made on that trip was the camp chef.

Time: 1 hour | Makes: 4 servings (1 large loaf)

DOUGH

2 AUS cups or 260 g or 2 US cups + 4 tsp self-raising (self-rising) flour

1 tsp salt

25 g (5 tsp) cold unsalted butter, chopped into rough cubes

½ AUS cup or 125 ml or ½ US cup + 1 tsp milk

½ AUS cup or 125 ml or ½ US cup + 1 tsp water

CORIANDER SEED HONEY

2 AUS tbsp or 7 g or 4 US tsp coriander seeds

½ AUS cup or 125 ml or ½ US cup + 1 tsp honey

½ tsp salt

½ tsp freshly ground black pepper

SERVING

150 g (10 US tbsp) butter (salted or unsalted, your preference)

Preheat the oven to 180°C (350°F), and place a Dutch oven or lined tray in the oven to preheat. Next, place the self-raising flour and salt in a large mixing bowl. Rub the cold butter into the flour with your fingers to combine into a sandy texture.

Carefully add the milk and water, using a fork to mix well. It may be easier to use your hands to continue kneading until all the liquid is absorbed and there are no dry pockets of flour left. Roughly form the dough into a large round. Place the dough in the Dutch oven or on the lined tray. Use a sharp knife to slash the top of the dough. Bake for 40 to 45 minutes until golden brown.

In the meantime, use the base of a heavy saucepan, a mortar and pestle or a spice grinder to coarsely grind the coriander seeds. Place the ground coriander seeds in a dry saucepan over medium-high heat and toast for 2 to 3 minutes, or until fragrant and darkened. Stir or shake the seeds frequently to prevent burning.

Add the honey, salt and pepper to the coriander seeds, stirring thoroughly to combine. Allow the honey to boil for 2 to 3 minutes over medium heat with the coriander seeds to infuse their flavour. Set aside to cool.

Serve the damper warm with generous lashings of butter and drizzles of coriander seed honey.

TIPS

» Carefully tap the bottom of the damper. If it sounds hollow, your damper is cooked through.

» You could replace self-raising flour with the same measure of plain (all-purpose) flour plus 2 teaspoons (9 g) of baking soda.

» Feel free to add any sweet or savoury ingredients, such as dried fruit or herbs, to the dough prior to baking.

» The damper is best eaten on the day of baking.

BEETROOT RAITA AND CHILLI OIL

Beetroots (beets) were not common in the food I ate growing up. You don't hear a lot of Malaysian or Chinese dishes featuring the earthy, wet, red vegetable. But the times I did eat beetroots, they were usually out of a tin and sliced super thin or grated to add to salad sandwiches or put on burgers (yep, that's a thing we do here in Australia—beetroot, eggs and pineapple rings all appear on our burgers). One of the most memorable times I did enjoy beetroot in Asian cuisine was at a more upscale restaurant serving a very contemporary take on Southern Indian and Sri Lankan cuisine. The beetroot came roasted in a mixture of whole cumin seeds, mustard seeds and drizzled with yoghurt. It was a delicious mix of earthy sweetness and creamy tanginess and that's exactly what this recipe captures. The drizzle of Lao Gan Ma Crispy Chilli Oil on top of this dip is absolutely necessary. It is an added texture and kick of spice that lifts the flavours.

Time: 1 hour | Makes: 4 servings

2 beetroots (total weight 320 g [about 11 oz]), washed thoroughly and patted dry, skin on

9 g (1½ tsp) salt, divided

4 AUS tbsp or 80 ml or ⅓ US cup neutral oil, divided

1 tsp ground cumin

1 tsp mustard seeds

2 AUS cups or 500 ml or 2 US cups + 2 US tbsp plain yoghurt

1 tsp freshly ground black pepper

½ tsp sugar

3 to 4 AUS tbsp or 60 to 80 ml or ¼ to ⅓ US cup Lao Gan Ma Crispy Chilli Oil

SERVING
Toasted pita chips

Preheat the oven to 190°C (375°F) and line a large, rimmed baking tray with parchment paper. Chop the beetroots into 2.5-cm (1-inch) pieces then mix them in a medium-sized bowl with ½ teaspoon of the salt and 1 AUS tablespoon (20 ml or 4 teaspoons) of the oil. Transfer the seasoned beetroot pieces to the tray and roast them in the oven for 40 to 45 minutes, tossing the beetroot pieces halfway through this time. The beetroots should be roasted until fork-tender.

Transfer the hot beetroot pieces to a food processor and blitz for 3 to 4 minutes, or until they form a coarse purée. Set aside.

In a small frying pan, heat the remaining 3 AUS tablespoons (60 ml or ¼ US cup) of neutral oil over medium heat. Once hot, add the cumin and mustard seeds. Toast for 1 to 2 minutes. Then remove the pan from the heat, keeping the cumin and mustard seeds in the pan, and allow to cool.

Mix together the cumin and mustard seeds in oil with the yoghurt, remaining teaspoon of salt, pepper, sugar and beetroot until fully incorporated. Transfer the raita to a serving dish. Garnish with drizzles of Lao Gan Ma Crispy Chilli Oil. Serve with toasted pita chips.

TIPS

» Beetroots can be peeled or unpeeled. The skin doesn't change the flavour or texture once cooked. I prefer peeled, as I like to use beetroot skins in other applications.

» Beetroot can be replaced with pumpkin or other squash or root vegetables.

» You can grate the beetroot instead of using a food processor.

ACKNOWLEDGMENTS

Aya, thank you. Your patience, gentleness, kindness and motivation have been the secret ingredients to this book. At times, grief seemed like an insurmountable wall, but your warmth and the space you created for my grief gave me courage and strength to overcome the heaviest of days. You have shown unwavering support, taken initiative and put in so much work without ever complaining. I am in awe.

Ben, I am so lucky to call you a friend and to get to work with you again on this journey. Thank you for your friendship, your honesty and your commitment. You go above and beyond, and I appreciate you immensely. Thank you for making this project fun, exciting, inspiring and full of colour. You have taught me to appreciate "a little mess" in the bigger picture.

To my friends, you are so important to me. You are so important to my creative process. The energy you share with me, the genuine interest you take in my work, the food we get to enjoy together, it is all pure joy. Thank you for bringing lightness to my life.

To the Page Street Publishing Team, thank you for your faith in me and your openness. I have loved working with you. To Emily Taylor, thank you for your patience, flexibility, positivity and attention to detail. You are so wonderful to work with.

ABOUT THE AUTHOR

Born and raised in Sydney, Australia, Sarah grew up in a Chinese-Malaysian family that loved to cook and eat. The dining table was where the family gathered to celebrate, share, commiserate, heal and grow together. The kitchen was always alive with the sound of sizzling, bubbling, spatulas clanging against the wok, the hiss of the pressure cooker releasing. The home always smelled of warm spices. Sarah and her mother shared a precious bond over food and ingredients. Food really was their love language. Sarah's extensive knowledge of ingredients, cooking techniques and confidence in the kitchen is by virtue of her relationship with her mother.

Sarah brings vibrant energy, excitement and bold flavours to her food and her events. Best known as one of *MasterChef Australia's* favourite finalists from 2017 and 2020, Sarah's passion for Southeast Asian cuisine and love of sharing food is a joy to watch and be a part of. Sarah is the successful author of the sensational cookbook *Sweet, Savory, Spicy* and owner of pop-up market stall Pork Party. Sarah's mastery of flavour and texture also comes to life through her cooking classes, online recipes and events.

Sarah can be found on social media:

Instagram: @fillmytummy

Facebook: facebook.com/sarahtiongau

YouTube: youtube.com/sarahtiong

INDEX